TOUCHING HEAVEN

DISCOVERING ORTHODOX CHRISTIANITY
ON THE ISLAND OF VALAAM

BY
JOHN OLIVER

CONCILIAR PRESS

Ben Lomond, California

TOUCHING HEAVEN:
Discovering Orthodox Christianity on the Island of Valaam
© Copyright 2003 by John Oliver

Published by   Conciliar Press
                  P.O. Box 76
                  Ben Lomond, California 95005-0076

Printed in the United States of America

ISBN 1-888212-65-9

All scripture quotations, unless otherwise indicated, are taken from the New King James Version. Copyright © 1979, 1980, 1982 by Thomas Nelson, Inc. Used by permission. All rights reserved.

Front cover photo: by Hierodeacon Savvaty, Valaam Monastery

Manufactured under the direction of Double Eagle Industries. For manufacturing details, call 888-824-4344 or e-mail to info@publishingquest.com

CONTENTS

BY FATHER JONAH PAFFHAUSEN

Valaam Monastery remains forever in my mind and heart. The silent islands amidst the sometimes placid, sometimes roaringly tempestuous waves of Lake Ladoga rise with forested cliffs like a beacon. Towering over them, visible for miles, is the great bell tower and church of the main monastery. The immense granite cross on the island of the Skete of St. John the Forerunner marks the otherness of that sacred place with a solidity that transcends this world. The other sketes, the forests with the ruined hermitages and dwellings of ancient ascetics, echo a life of sanctity and beauty of which this world has no consciousness.

It is not simply the place, though. The monastery is not the buildings or the institution. Nor is it the exquisite church services, their majestic austerity, the hymns glorifying God and stirring repentance and compunction, echoing in the cavernous temples. The monastery is the people, the community, the fathers. Through ascetic labors the fathers of the monastery strive to bring themselves under complete control through spiritual effort, being purified, enlightened, deified. Their efforts have one goal, to remove all barriers to love of God and neighbor. These are men filled with grace, striving after grace, struggling with themselves to overcome all barriers to that grace, which is itself the love of God.

5

A monastery is a place of spiritual struggle, of purification through trials and temptations. Wherever grace and sanctity are, so will there be trials and temptations in the same measure. My life at Valaam was one permeated with temptations, struggles, trials; for by dealing with these temptations, one works out one's salvation, one learns how to cease reacting to the provocations from others, from one's own passions, from the world. One comes to realize that the tempter is real, and that he exploits our weaknesses and shortcomings. But through those often bitter lessons, one comes to a more profound awareness of grace, of the tangible Presence of God.

Truly Valaam is a dwelling place of God.

I became a novice at Valaam in the summer of 1993 and was there for about six months. As I already had an extensive theological education, mine was not a usual kind of novitiate. And being a Westerner with a background in finance, I had some skill that others there did not. So I was assigned to work with the abbot, Archimandrite Pankratiy, on business and missionary ventures of the community, and in dealing with foreign visitors.

I joined the community after finding in Fr. Pankratiy a true friend and brother, one with whom I shared the same vision of the Church and of the monastic life, and one in whom I could see who and what I wanted to become. He is only a few years older than I, and I esteem him profoundly as a father in Christ. He in turn led me to others—to his own elder, Archimandrite Kyrill of the Trinity-St. Sergius Lavra, who blessed my path as a hieromonk; and to Fr. Raphael, the wonderful elder whom Fr. Pankratiy had known in the Caucasus, and who had come to Valaam at his invitation. I'll never forget that first life confession with Fr. Raphael when I was received as a novice. I confessed to him the sins I remembered and knew; and then he took over, telling me of the sins I had not remembered to confess, those unknown and those I had tried to hide. This began my relationship with him, and would become a foundation of healing for the rest of my life.

Father Pankratiy had taken over the abbacy at Valaam in February of 1993. Monks had been there for about four years, but the place was still mostly ruined, inhabited by Soviet villagers who had sunk into the most decrepit poverty and destitution. The community was rife with issues of zealotry and a great uncertainty as to how to go about the task of reconstructing a great institution, from the buildings to the inner life of the community, after seventy-five years of desolation. There were about fifty men then, in various stages of monastic commitment, mostly novices. The main complex was only partially in the hands of the brotherhood, and the sketes were mostly ruins.

I had seriously intended to stay at Valaam long-term. When Russia looked to be on the brink of civil war, with the shelling of their own parliament building, we reevaluated this intention with the help of an eldress near St. Petersburg. It was determined that I could help the monastery far more from America than by being present there as just one more hieromonk with a funny accent. So I returned home in late November, soon to be ordained as a deacon, trying to find support for Valaam and its rebuilding efforts, and with hopes of establishing an American branch of Valaam in California.

I returned to Valaam in February of 1994. Fr. Pankratiy had an idea, to fulfill a need and provide an opportunity for a working pilgrimage: A group of Americans would raise some money for materials, come to Valaam, and build a building. We fleshed this out and conceived a plan to bring two groups, successively for three weeks each, to construct a building at the Skete of St. John the Forerunner. The groups would raise the money, and the monastery would buy all the materials. And the groups would get tours of Moscow and St. Petersburg in the process. But what we hoped for, without realizing how great it would be, was the impact of the experience of the monastery on the pilgrims.

The community that came together for this was quite remarkable. There was a large contingent from the recently converted Antiochian Evangelical Orthodox Mission, with several priests from various parts of the country and many young people. Then there were people from the broad spectrum of the Orthodox community in America, from several jurisdictions, and some on the fringes of the Church. For all, it was a life-changing event.

It was not simply the experience of camping on an island that had been inhabited by the most severe ascetics of the Russian North, sanctified by their sweat, labors, and graves. It was not simply being exposed to the services in the main monastery on weekends, the great Saturday night vigil, from one to eight in the morning. I can still hear the immense bell, echoing in my memory, across the miles of lake and islands. It was not just the ascetic sacrifice of time and labor to rebuild this hermitage, nor even the visit of His Holiness, Patriarch Alexei II, blessing the workers and the foundations.

The experience that transformed most people was the encounter with Fr. Raphael. I had the blessing to be his translator, and thus had the immense blessing to benefit from all the advice given to each, to see how he dealt with each person uniquely and could see their zeal, their love, their pain— even despite my poor efforts at translation. And in him, through him, each one, to some degree, encountered the Living Christ. Fr. Raphael, by his joy and humility, his wisdom and clairvoyance, showed each one that Orthodox Christianity works. It produces elders, living saints, who embrace each one with the love of Christ. It showed us what monasticism, what Christianity, is all about.

—Hieromonk Jonah
Abbot of the Monastery of St. John of
Shanghai and San Francisco
Point Reyes, California

ENTERING WONDER

D eep in a northern Russian forest of jade and brown, far from any hint of civilization, Valaam Monastery sinks into the seasons of the year as it has for a thousand years before. Nearly one hundred monks labor in this place that rests on an island over 100 miles north of St. Petersburg, and an immeasurable distance from the Western world. Valaam is accessible only by ferryboats that must cross wide Lake Ladoga, and the lake isn't always cooperative. The trees, plants, animals, water, air, soil, and the whole life cycle here in this wilderness flourish without much stain from over-population or industry. It is quiet here, and these quiet roots run deep. The paradox of Valaam is that this place is peaceful but not without violence.

In our world, the treasure of stillness requires a fierce guarding. Remember, it is not a flimsy sign but a flaming sword that protects the Garden of Eden. The Gospel according to St. Matthew puts it best: "From the days of John the Baptist until now the kingdom of heaven suffers violence, and the violent take it by force" (11:12). One traditional interpretation of that verse is that the Christian life is not for the faint of heart. The renunciation of self, the taking up of one's cross, the salvation work of "fear and trembling" (Philippians 2:12)—these are

11

soldier-images that suggest a disciplined struggle is needed if we are to enter fully into the journey of defeat and victory that is the Christian life. Defeat can bring humility, and victory, joy. The monks at Valaam are a band of fierce fighters who sing and pick wildflowers. When I stayed at the monastery, the fullness of life there revealed some gaping holes in my own.

I was told to "enter in" to the monastic cycle of services. As a young American, I do not "enter in," I observe . . . cautiously. But I did what I could as often as I could with as much devotion as my feeble spirit could produce. It took a few days to lay down my resistance and accept that this is how they do things here. Indeed, this is how they have always done things: wake with the sun, offer prayers in the church, eat, labor; more prayers, more labor, a bit more food, a walk in the woods, more prayers into the night. The Christian year is built upon the Christian day, which is built upon the Christian hour and the Christian moment. When it was time to pray, we prayed. When it was time to eat, we ate. When it was time to play, we played. The civil war between what my spirit craved and what my flesh would settle for eased as the days passed. Monastic life has a rhythm, and I wanted to learn it. Or, at least, I wanted to absorb enough of it so that I would never forget it, but spend the rest of my life trying to get it back. It's a bit like pruning a small shoot off a plant and then planting the shoot in soil elsewhere so that it will grow into a life of its own.

Then, a key thing happened during the Divine Liturgy one Sunday morning—during the Little Entrance, that moment when the Gospel is carried in the uplifted hands of the priest before the people. The church is dark and cool. Candlelight illuminates the smoke of incense into silver scarves stretching toward the ceiling. There is quiet movement around the long cement room as candles are lit and icons are venerated by monks, novices, pilgrims, and residents of a small village nearby. Then there is the chanting; this music that has been seasoned by centuries of honored use resonates within my deepest places. I stand very still. The chant, so beautiful, is offered as one sound, no monk louder than another. The language of the service is Slavonic, but in this moment we are deeper than language. The door on the far left of the iconostasis opens and the monks and celebrants bring the Gospel into the view of the people. The people bow; I strain my neck to observe. And there is the difference.

Our culture in America is in a passionate love affair with itself. An unbridled pursuit of personal happiness and a worship of individualism have spawned a worldview inadequate to receive the mysteries of God. I am a product of this culture and have sacrificed myself to it. Its worldview discolors my own. Certainly there are good and honorable qualities of our culture, but they are not the qualities toward which I naturally gravitate. I am thoroughly American in that life is lived on my terms; I am emphatically Christian in that I believe it shouldn't be. Rebellion, of course, respects no geography; it is present in all humans everywhere. But as I've studied the Holy Scriptures, for example, I have noticed my tendency to want to master, rather than to be mastered. Consider this passage from *The Communion of Love* by Matthew the Poor, a monk and spiritual father in the Monastery of St. Macarius in the Egyptian desert:

> There are two ways of reading [the Holy Scriptures]: The first is when a man reads and puts himself and his mind in control of the text, trying to subject its meaning to his own understanding and then comparing it with the understanding of others. The second is when

a man puts the text on a level above himself and tries to bring his mind into submission to its meaning, and even sets the text up as a judge over him, counting it as the highest criterion.[1]

Notice the difference? When I come to the Word of God on my own terms, I am trapped in misguided questions: "How do *I* feel about this?" "What does this do for *me*?" "How does this satisfy *my* understanding?" "What argument can *I* win with this information?" If my desire to learn and apply the practical truths of Holy Scripture is disconnected from the Holy Tradition of the Church and left to my own clever thinking, it can deteriorate into treating the Bible as the brightest gold on my throne or the heaviest weapon in my arsenal. But here at Valaam, in the precious hush of the ancient Divine Liturgy, the Holy Scriptures were held high above bowed heads and bent knees. These Orthodox Christians chose the only attitude appropriate for a people before their God—humility. And as an Orthodox Christian living in an American culture where humility is dismissed as a sign of weakness, I was blessed with the sacred exposure to another way of doing things.

The violence at Valaam Monastery is the violence of spiritual warfare. And it is the violence I will carry with me when I leave Valaam, if I ever want to live at peace with God, with my neighbor, and with myself. It is the renunciation of those selfish parts of myself so that I may become more like the loving Christ; it is the taking up of my cross so that the comfort of the Holy Spirit is made known; it is the salvation work of laying down my arrogance so that I may draw near to the Holy Scriptures in the context of the Church, the way a dying man draws near to the only medicine that can save him. I do not have a clear sense of how to do this, of how to become this man of whom I have caught a glimpse at the monastery. I do know, however, that it begins with learning how to bow in humility to the Lord Jesus rather than straining my neck to observe all the interesting things He can do for me.

As the monks and celebrants carry the Gospel to the altar, I shift my weight from one foot to the other. This is the eighth consecutive hour of services, and in traditional Orthodox churches there are no pews. Benches line the walls of the nave for the elderly and infirm and those who need a break from standing. But most of us stand; we stand like soldiers.

I observe the old women, the *babushki*—who, thrice my age, have none of my impatience. I observe the aroma of the incense that is the dried sap of those ancient trees outside. I observe the candles that give light to the church and that shine with the names of people offered in prayer to God, some of whom are praying for us. I observe the icons, the windows of heaven, that give detail to the faces of saints, and I wonder if they observe me. The Liturgy carries on peacefully and invites each of us to participate in the worship of God. I reflect for a moment that at one time in church history, a man could not become a bishop unless he knew the entire Book of Psalms by heart. "Well," I think to myself, "I might know a couple of psalms." I decide it is time to stop thinking. I decide it is time to "enter in."

CHAPTER 1

TAPESTRY AND FAMILY

We are often unable to see our own stories in the making. But in reflective moments, we see our stories lying like tapestries behind us and notice how individual threads of experiences, of decisions, of persons whose paths crossed ours, weave a life that is our life. I remember my plane ride to Moscow for the Valaam trip; in fact, I remember remembering. As I stared through the window of seat 22-J, I took an inventory of the threads of my life that offered some explanation as to why I was headed for a monastery on the other side of the world. Taking an inventory is risky, I thought, because of the temptation toward self-importance. It is one thing to reflect on the evidence of God's guidance in my life; it is another to take credit for it.

The reflection was worth the risk. My story is peppered with gifts and graces from God, both joyful and painful, that appeared often when I was most unaware of my need for them. My family is one of those joyful and painful gifts. I am not sure anyone really remembers his childhood accurately, but images do linger: a small yellow house on a short suburban street with a driveway that seemed to stretch into the next town; chasing an older sister whose approval was more cherished than toys; reaching for a five-dollar bill from the large, wrinkled hand of a grandfather. I searched my past for the seeds that had grown into this current hunger for an experience like Valaam, where issues that we all face, such as identity and rootedness, might receive some needed clarity. Some seeds—of my hunger, and of the issues—were found scattered among the relationships in my family.

Certainly a strong image rich with emotional detail is a photograph I have of my parents, my sister, and me taken when I was two or three years old. The fading print shows my father, a historian, standing behind a couch where the other three are seated, his hands resting on the back of the couch. My mother, leaning away from my father, is holding me in her lap. In contrast to her quiet elegance is my "deer-in-the-headlights" expression that kids get when a flashbulb goes off. My sister, restless with toy in hand, sits to our left on the edge of the couch. The photograph carries a hint of an early uneasiness, a kind of subtle groping for an understanding of our roles and relationships. Our home often had an invigorating atmosphere that comes from loving the life of the mind, for both my parents were book-lovers. But in all the grammar and arithmetic, we lost a precious intimacy with each other. Attempts at true knowing were made, of course, but without enough selflessness to become habitual.

I felt this struggle between my father and mother, even though much of their suffering was done in private. They lost each other in the years, then gave up looking. The hardening, the exhaustion from shattering each other's ideals, was too strong to do no damage.

My father was a leading evangelical in the community during my childhood, and I remember our doors were often darkened by men and women who brought fascinating conversation with them. My mother would move along the fringes of these living room conversations, aware but uncomfortable. She poured the coffee out of duty while quietly fighting her own battles. Her struggle, no less serious for being quiet, came from not knowing who she was while knowing too well what others wanted her to be. And when she did catch glimpses of who she thought she was, she didn't always find that person worth loving.

We see this struggle around us; we see it in us. We get used to struggling quietly and do not notice that we've drifted into isolation. The four of us lived in a large house of many hidden spaces, and now I see that perhaps that wasn't such a good thing.

As I considered these threads of my story while on the plane to Moscow, I reached for a pen and paper. A quotation from St. Augustine drifted to mind and I thought it pertinent enough to keep it handy. As he considered his own threads, he wrote: "Thou hast made us for Thyself, and our hearts find no peace until they rest in Thee."[2]

I wonder if I still have that piece of paper somewhere. Perhaps it lies with that old family photograph, or with a twenty-year-old letter from my father trying to explain the mess. Or perhaps it lies in the pages of one of my dusty books on Zen Buddhism or Native American spirituality. More likely, it is a lost bookmark in whatever magazine I'd been reading to pass the time between musings, as the huge silver bird droned on toward the coming night.

CHAPTER 2

FUMBLING TOWARD FAITH

We have popular words to describe our searches for rootedness. In religious circles, "pilgrims" have their "pilgrimages," "sojourners" have their "journeys." It's attractive language, really, not only because it sounds pretty, but hidden inside that kind of talk might lie our comfortable excuses to be noncommittal. When I grew old enough to use that language with any credibility—say, my college years—my search for identity was fueled by a tangle of motives. I wanted security as much as I wanted rootedness, and I discovered that they aren't always the same. Years before my introduction to monasticism, I sought a resting place among the belief systems I encountered—sometimes just wanting shelter, sometimes wanting a home.

The Christian faith makes a curious bequest. A child inherits a pantheon of great stories and giant heroes, of gardens and serpents, of paradise and perdition. And like fingerprints on old parchment, he receives not just the stories, but also the ways in which those stories were interpreted by his progenitors. I was blessed in that all this mythology was handed to me with enough care, enough discipline and demonstration, to help me believe that it was all true. I have always believed it to be true; but as a young man I often wondered if it was unique.

The Christian stories may be perfect, but the people who pass them on aren't. So we receive the parchment of faith with fingerprints obscuring some very important parts of the Story. The longing for an eraser sends us searching.

The Christian schools I attended did the very best with their meager resources. They are securely among my finest memories. But I noticed there an easy tendency to replace mystery with monsters. Often, that pantheon of edifying and terrifying Christian stories was scrubbed clean of its mystery and crammed into something comprehensible, digestible, and, by inference, controllable. After all, the primal, the dark, the sexual, the dangerous, the wild, all these simmer in the shadows of mystery. Naturally, then, we students were schooled in a drastically diminished Bible.

Over time, though, the right messages took root. I never abandoned the Christian worldview—perhaps in behavior, not in belief—but I drifted for a time toward Zen Buddhism and a few Native American spiritualities rather than toward the spit-shined guarantees of the faith of my youth. Zen drew me in because of its respect for mystery, Native American spirituality because of its respect for the earth. In my wandering I discovered that a faith only of the mind is no faith indeed, because it lacks *faithfulness*. For too many years, my God was the God of the books. It was that tangle of motives: drifting through these belief systems because I was searching for a home, but also because drifting means never having to settle down. It is easier to admire the demands of the spiritual life when one is too undisciplined to obey them.

My first encounter with monasticism was not in a Christian brotherhood or secluded convent, but in the pages of Zen texts. It was that deep undercurrent of blessed monotony that attracted me to monastic life. The rootedness I lost in the brokenness of my family was to be found there, and the singularity of purpose seemed a refreshing alternative to my spiritual discipline, which was about as substantive and permanent as smoke in the wind. These, though, were secret epiphanies. In the hearts and minds of those who knew me, there would be no sympathy for either these ancient Eastern principles or my awkward attempts to apply them. Even in my conscience, informed as it was by the voices of a thousand who have helped and harmed, there was deep conflict. Can there be such a thing, I wondered, as a Zen Christian?

These ideas and struggles, these habits and inheritances, I carried with me to the autumn of 1987, when a chastening but necessary experience crumbled the foundation of some of my old living. I had returned to Ohio to attend a Quaker college and, while sifting through my limited career options, had gained employment as a youth minister at a church. One afternoon in his study, the pastor mentioned that he would be out of town one Sunday next month and that the responsibility of preaching the morning sermon fell on the next clergy member. In this church, there were two clergy members. On that Sunday, one would be out of town, the other would see a precious opportunity to be—finally—the son of a proud father, to drink deeply the rare air that surrounds leadership, to discard at last the clinging, awkward coat of adolescence.

On that morning, the sun transformed the sanctuary's thin dust clouds into trails of incense smoke falling inward from the windows. After the congregation was seated, this twenty-year-old preacher and four elders of the church walked down the aisle, which, up to this moment, had never seemed so gloriously long. In my maroon sweater and shoulder-length hair, I rested on the throne reserved for important tasks like this, for important men like me. As I ascended into the pulpit to preach my sermon, I avoided eye contact with anyone who might know me well enough to witness the spectacle taking place before them. For on that morning, I did what no one who has such limited experience with this subject should ever do: I preached a sermon about suffering. And I loved them all for loving me after.

In some belief systems it is known as "the way of the ascender." It is the path often taken by old boys struggling to become ageless, mythological men. It is the way of those who seek to satisfy an appetite for *prominence.*

The hunger for prominence, to be sure, is encouraged by our culture, but also strangely encouraged by our culture's popular Christian worldview. One dangerous consequence of our preoccupation with celebrity is that now every kid wants to be one. Rugged individualism is rewarded with the attention needed to sustain it. But in this dark circle, we find traces of support from a popular spirituality that is inherently structured around the idea of the "hero." Leadership is crucial, of course, and so is grooming the young to provide a strong kind. But we who take the shortcut of personality to avoid the long and hard road of character; we who pose with all the answers and underestimate mystery; we who define "soul work" not as reciting the Jesus prayer while digging in the garden, but as jockeying to lead a Bible study; and we who live as if prominence were one of the gifts of the Holy Spirit—we are the ascenders. And we are heading in the wrong direction.

In the months and years after descending from that pulpit, there were awkward but true attempts to go in a different direction. One deep undercurrent of this time was the need just to be quiet. I felt small tugs away from prominence and an urge toward a more realistic and honest condition of waiting. None of these sensations was very recognizable at the time;

it is with hindsight that I reflect now. I especially consider those moments when I felt on the edge of breathing pure mystery. Yes, they were few. But who is so great a God as our God, who honors genuine striving toward Him with moments when mystery has meaning and life is pregnant with astonishing joy? If only I could see the ordinary as that mysterious.

And then the phone rang.

CHAPTER 3

AWAKENING TO ORTHODOXY

The dull monotony of drifting rootlessly among relationships and religions was interrupted by the ring of my telephone one Thursday morning. My father was calling with a simple invitation. Apparently, in a pro-life gathering and its subsequent meetings, he had become acquainted with an Orthodox Christian priest. As far as he could tell, I should meet this man. My father—a man of words—admitted to not really knowing how to describe Father David. So he resorted to a word he uses when he wants to tide his listener over until a more comprehensive appraisal is formed: "Father David is . . . charming." I was tided over, but grew curious.

Orthodoxy? Catholicism from another part of the world, right? I had had several encounters with highly liturgical churches before this phone call. While attending school in Seattle, I frequented a Compline service at a Roman Catholic church on weekday evenings. Nice chanting, neat smells, great study breaks. I often caught a ride with two friends who were fans of hard rock music—loud, throbbing, window-melting hard rock music. More than once we lingered in the parking lot to absorb the shock of the last few minutes of some sonic bombast before entering the church. The sanctuary was supposed to be silent for awhile, but I did not hear silence. I heard the echoes of screams.

In those times when I attended Compline alone, though, I heard something else. There—my raincoat-covered body poured into an old wooden pew—I heard a few notes of the mystery of worship. Deep-voiced chanting of ancient texts lingered on candle flames and reached into every corner in need of light. At that time in my life, the divine melody didn't have a prayer against the dark choir of the world, the flesh, and the devil. But with the ancient music of God, a few notes are sufficient to leave a person with a hunger to hear more.

My father arranged for a breakfast meeting with Father David and me on a Saturday morning. I carried that dull film that clings to musicians when we're disturbed before noon. Father David, however, was obviously used to early mornings. The language of his body—a shape he calls "circumferentially challenged"—and his tone of voice seemed at ease with the day so far and our moment in it. Our conversation lasted till the lunch hour, and by that time I had learned enough of Orthodoxy to want to learn more.

"Who are your influences, John?"

"Um, St. Augustine."

"I see. That's pretty much when we think things started to go wrong."

And so it went. What a curious fellow he was, with a comfortable balance of holiness and humor. His ability to good-naturedly offend—leaving his victim flustered but feeling no need to retaliate—was highly evolved. Yet we exchanged something more that morning than random clues to our stories, because I remember leaving our encounter restless and without words to explain why.

The Orthodox priest extended invitations to visit his

church and borrow books from his library. I sensed from spending time in that church that a smooth and worn path lay between the library and the nave. An almost palpable quality to the parish was that its members seemed to possess both spiritual literacy and love for its services. At least, most of those I met had both; some, literacy or love. But these encounters amounted to a stirring example of a people who do more than attend the church—they act like the Church.

In the months prior to meeting Father David, I had wandered that life-draining wasteland that waits for anyone who wildly hungers for truth, but who does everything he can to avoid it. What makes it draining, I think, is our reluctance to recognize just why we evade that which we desire, and our powerlessness to ease the pain that lingers as a result. St. Paul, in his letter to the Christians in Rome, noted his struggle with these tendencies when he lamented that "the good that I will to do, I do not do" (7:19). Perhaps it is when we sabotage our pursuit of what is good and right and noble that the reality of our rebellion becomes most obvious—in the same way that our need for light becomes more obvious the deeper we sink into the shadows. What a bothersome consequence of the fall of man.

The footsteps of my journey toward the Orthodox Christian Church helped deepen the groove of the path between the library and the nave of Father David's church. I don't remember him ever handing me a book without also extending an invitation to observe worship. That seemed to be the deal—a book for a service. In fact, attending the services, he said, would be a light unto my path superior to a title or two on theology. Books are valuable, to be sure, but the whole of the Orthodox Church services is the real treasure. Books help but they do not replace. Overlook our small congregation's frail and mortal contributions to the Liturgy, he suggested, and you'll see the Church that covers the centuries.

On that cold and gray January day in 1991, after breakfast with my dad and Father David, I did begin reading and attending, reading and attending. Like the organic rhythm of faith and works, the books I read led me deeper into the services I attended, and the services I attended led me deeper into the books I read. It is in a sacred cycle such as this that one discovers that the rational and the mysterious are, in fact, old friends. But attending the services leveled a greater shock to my Protestant sensibility than reading about them, for the same reason that leaping into a dark and cold river renders benign a book about swimming. What was this world into which I was experientially stumbling?

I had known the god who exists only in the vacuous universe between the page and the mind. Many were the moments when I was afraid of the silence in a room or the whisper in my soul, and nervously reached for a book *about* the God who might be trying to confront me, precisely so that I could avoid confronting Him. Yes, illumination comes at the hands of those who not only know about God, but truly *know* Him, and share Him with us in a book. But something happens to impair our openness when we reach for a book not as a doorway into deeper understanding, but as a distraction. Our soul takes a subtle wrong turn, and we wind up still looking over some hill or across some field at the place where we really need to be.

So this journey, shepherded by a priest and his parishioners, carried me deep into territory I had assumed inconsequential until now. For several months we wandered the dusty roads of the early Church: What happened to these people and to their Faith after the ink dried on the last passages of the

Holy Scriptures? We lingered in the company of saints whose choices reveal the staggering differences between life and "abundant" life: Who were these men and women and what have they to do with me?

When summer came, we rode hard through the Protestant brushwood I had inherited and taken as my own: What is trustworthy and believable, and what is dangerous and soul-destroying? We traveled through the spiritual disciplines of Orthodoxy that lead to salvation: How does our cooperation with Christ manifest itself in everyday life? We moved reverently through ancient and modern monasteries ignored by the faith of my youth: Why had these treasures been discarded and forgotten? Have the monks and nuns gone there to escape the world, or to confront it in themselves?

Much of our journey happened in the quiet fellowship hall next to the church, where we would sip hot tea after morning services and talk. On the Sundays I didn't attend the Orthodox church, I'd visit either a Quaker church or a mildly charismatic gathering, or I would sleep in. But I came to Father David with a restless mind and a soul bruised by trendy spiritual techniques that didn't work. And I came without a clear idea of what I was looking for; I just knew I was looking.

The journey had a stirring deeper than consciousness. Like the pulsing world that lay beneath the surface of the sea—with its cycles of life and death—the fundamental shifts needed to change a person happened imperceptibly. There were no fireworks; there was no parade. That I didn't have a grand cosmic experience, as a saint might, was obvious—for I was not a saint—and even saints don't go looking for grand cosmic experiences. But what I did notice were subtle changes in my thinking, in my behavior, in the patterns of thought from which I made my choices and perceived my neighbor.

When I gathered enough reflective moments, an image emerged of what all this was doing to me. That uneasy sense of having no *home* that for so long hung on me like a wet ragged cloak began to fall slowly from my shoulders. The heaviness of not knowing who one really is and where one really belongs—of having no identity and no rootedness—hangs on the soul and weighs it down: the body loses confidence; worthy dreams never come to fruition; relationships sag with awkwardness; no resolve exists to draw boundaries around one's soul and hang a banner warning those who would run roughshod, "Tread Lightly." Notice, though, that the wet ragged coat was falling slowly and gradually. True soul work is unhurried, deep, mundane.

The year of books and conversations and services and reflections was drawing to an anxious close. I remember a pallid autumn Sunday, walking toward my car, receiving these haunting words from Father David: "I'm sorry, but you're in a dangerous time." To turn away now might be a retreat into ignorance and, therefore, bring some possibility of divine pardon. But another step or two closer toward the Orthodox Church would be a step or two into that Light for which I would be responsible and from which I could never hide. The Apostle Peter must have been familiar with these moments of decision, for in his second epistle he affirms that it would be "better . . . not to have known the way of righteousness, than having known it, to turn from" it (2:21). Some knowledge comes with an exacting price.

For a short while, I stopped attending Father David's church. The swirl of ideas and demands and uncertainties was overwhelming, and I needed time to sort through and scrutinize them all. Or so I thought. While the stir and froth of my rational faculties was making lots of noise, another quieter sound was calling. I noticed that while my assumptions were being challenged, my heart was being changed. Softened. The truth was being revealed not only in ways comprehensible, but in a kind of soul-language that engaged the whole of me. I discovered that I wasn't meditating on the Orthodox Church; the Orthodox Church was meditating on me.

In January of 1991, I drew a deep, anticipating breath; in December of that year, I just as deeply exhaled and settled—finally, after much searching—into a place of resolution. My mother and I were driving to Ohio after a Christmas visit with my grandparents in Florida. While on a stretch of Highway 19 that threads a portion of West Virginian Appalachian mountains, I sank into the sweetness that emerged from remembering all the summers I had spent there hiking and whitewater rafting. Each river and trail took a turn offering up its share of memories. Any tension I felt from the long trip eased, and the natural defenses of my personality lowered. Feeling safe and soulful, I made my decision.

I could not believe in all of it, so I believed in what I could. And for every answer that the Orthodox Church provided, another question took its place. I ran through the carnival of ideas in my head as we rolled through the mountains at sunset. If scrutinized in isolated pieces, there was plenty in the Church I did not understand. But I sensed that this was not the way to look at the Church. My reasoning abilities were flawed anyway, so my conclusions wouldn't be entirely reliable. No, the best way for me to consider the Church was to come to it not on my terms, but on its terms.

And that meant discarding not the world I encountered, but much of the lens through which I encountered the world. It meant letting go of my preconceptions, the ones informed by a Protestant worldview suspicious of any spiritual expression resembling Catholicism, and dismissive of most of Christian history before the Reformation. It meant reevaluating *sola fide*—the Protestant assertion that *only faith* is necessary for salvation. This assertion shoved me toward two erring tendencies: to relegate faith to the theater of the mind, where it lacks clear definition and, therefore, clear expression; or to conform to the shifting doctrinal winds of the latest faith "revival" or the newest faith "movement." Surely, *sola fide* is often censured simplistically, but in my experience I had seen it segregated and lifted above any proper framework. All in all, coming to the Church on its terms meant throwing away the old wineskins.

The Orthodox Church is a worshipping Church. The mystery of worship is its reality. Worship is a prism through which we creatures honor our Creator in the midst of His creation, and He curiously honors us back. Far from being an isolated spiritual transaction, worship colors all of life. When the Apostle Paul, in the first chapter of Romans, lists so much of what is wrong with the world, he traces the whole cosmic illness back to us humans forsaking our roles as worshipping beings—*homo adorans*—and as beings of thankfulness. The term "Orthodox" literally means "right worship" or "right belief." The Church nudges worship into every corner and crack of life, from its most mysterious to its most ordinary.

Considered, then, in this context of worship as a relational experience between man and God, each issue within the Church I found difficult to accept began revealing itself to be a deeper part of an organic whole. The task was not to step forward and scrutinize, for example, the Sacrament of Confession in a kind of intellectual quarantine, but to step back and discover how through confession a person is cleansed and restored to his place as a worshipping being. The Church was revealed to be deeply therapeutic—not in the modern ego-centric sense of that word, but as the true Body of Christ, who came to heal the soul and mind and body.

At last, I understood that I could no longer live a life of deference to the two most destructive forces found in modern spirituality—isolated effort and unbridled freedom. No, I needed to summon a higher allegiance if I were to receive the truth of who I am and where I belong, if I were to discover my true identity and rootedness. I was called to be servant in the House of the Father and the Son and the Holy Spirit; I was called to be an Orthodox Christian.

The first Sunday after my return to Ohio, I made it a point to see Father David in his study. We exchanged enough conversation for him to discern I was ready to be baptized. "Whatever you have learned to be good, to be true, to be holy," he advised, "bring those things home with you." My baptism was not just the renouncing of my devotion to the untrue things in my past; it was the fulfillment of the true things I received along the way.

Sunday morning, the twelfth of January, 1992. On the narthex floor of the small church, a newly purchased cattle trough served as our baptismal, and great fun was had at my expense. My family was given seats of honor, which meant the only seats with a full view in the midst of onlookers. I had enough of an understanding of the significance of baptism to see the trough as both a coffin and a womb. Kneeling in the trough, I was gripped in the experienced hands of Father David and submerged forward three times. As the water fell off my body in a thousand clear splashes, my soul came to its home, ready to begin a new journey.

CHAPTER 4

FROM ROUTINE TO RUSSIA

A Zen proverb observes that "when the student is ready, the teacher will appear." I like that. The proverb has the ring of mystery to it—like when the character Evangelist appears suddenly and without introduction to the desperate Christian in John Bunyan's *Pilgrim's Progress*. Teachers appear in the vestments of a priest, in the lofty speech of a poet, and in the stench of a homeless alcoholic. They hide in the truths of stories and in the wake of tragedies. When we are alert and open—when we are ready—they instruct with power.

My next teacher appeared in the last four pages of a magazine. While living in Florida in 1994, I received in the mail my monthly copy of a magazine about Orthodox Christianity. According to habit, I paged through the issue with the resolution of reading every article, but managed to read just a few. The final article in the magazine was about a monastery in Russia and was written with such skill as to communicate the author's love for Valaam Monastery and for the architectural renovations happening there. Because of an unstable economy and a political climate aggressively hostile towards Christian Tradition, Valaam had fallen into decay. Current efforts to renovate portions of the monastery and its chapels were chronicled in the article. Photographs of the monastery and its abbot accompanied the moving text.

It could have been a simple need for change, or an ache to participate in the kind of purposeful living described in the article. But the *experience* of monastic life—about which I knew so little and previously couldn't have cared less—hit me with a quiet force. Valaam Monastery stayed with me for days. I read the article again to pick up other nuances, other details that might help enrich an emerging mental image. Finally, I decided to locate the author to express my appreciation.

James was, at the time, a deacon serving an Orthodox church in California.* His connection with Valaam Monastery was significant, for he was considered a "brother" of the community and would occasionally serve as a deacon when visiting. As a result of his additional comments on monastic life and the renovation efforts during our conversation, I began to feel personally connected to this ancient place and to these brave men. Then, the deacon surprised me: "We're putting together a pilgrimage to Valaam to help with the renovation. Would you be interested in going?" The student was ready, and the teacher had appeared.

Several months of fund-raising and fact-finding hurried by. A passport and visa and really good socks all needed a place in my backpack. The transition from an uneventful existence with family to the aggressive sport of world travel felt sudden, but refreshing. And the anticipation was extraordinary as I left Florida for Helsinki, Finland, in June of 1994. A journal entry for Day One describes the experience:

---

*Deacon James is now Father Jonah, author of the Foreword to this book. It is common Orthodox practice for a man to receive a new name upon ordination to the priesthood or upon monastic profession.

This plane, with its cargo of tongues from other worlds, departed from Miami about thirty minutes ago. Already I've heard from America, Finland, Puerto Rico, and Germany. . . . There's a slight exhilaration in being in the minority, a slight uneasiness perhaps. A television monitor hangs above a partition that separates the cabins in the fuselage. The facts of our flight— airspeed, distance to destination, altitude, destination local time, and probability of a nasty plane crash—are displayed first in English, then Finnish. . . . There seem to be many other voices, too. These are internal voices, all vying for my attention. All of them are different but all are mine. My soul is restless in trying to be an audience for all of them.

My first brush with trouble on this trip occurred when I arrived at the Moscow airport. Hundreds of travelers were ushered off planes and routed through customs. I was one of the first to funnel into the small aisle to present my passport and visa for inspection. Ensconced in a small booth, the customs officer scrutinized my visa for a minute or so. The skin on his face was waging war with teenage acne, and the skin was losing. I guessed his age to be no greater than twenty, but he bullied with experience beyond his years.

In clear fresh tones, he barked a sentence at me in Russian while pointing to my visa. I shrugged my shoulders and raised my eyebrows in response. My visa, I surmised, was no good. His gestures suggested that it had the wrong entry date. I felt certain he would reach for the rifle hanging by his side to explain the matter in very different terms. Yep, this was Russia; this was the land vilified by the popular culture back home in America. When Hollywood or Washington, D.C., needed an enemy, it was usually Russia. Suspicion rushed between this young officer and me.

He managed a few words in English. Yes, in fact, the entry date was off by one day. I was not allowed to enter the country. Tension mounted as I said nothing. Finally, he leaned into the glass toward me, lowered his voice and said, "Fifty dollars makes it okay." I glanced to my left to see a swelling crowd of anxious travelers, all wanting just to get through customs and go home. The officer, too, was getting anxious. Just as I was ready to barter that price down to twenty dollars, he swiftly reared back, stamped the visa in frustration, and signaled for me to pass. My, I thought to myself, this trip is starting well.

After spending the night on the floor of the Moscow airport, I joined Deacon James and the other pilgrims. We spent several days in Moscow touring Orthodox churches—churches with bricks and mortar older than our entire American civilization. Russian culture displays a curious paradox: although much of its citizenry struggles with drunkenness, most of its churches worship in sobriety—a sobriety that abstains not from alcohol, but from sloth. Peasants and professionals alike showed remarkable self-discipline in their worship activities—standing quietly during the services, fighting tiredness, assuming a kind of physical humility when lighting a candle, venerating an icon, or receiving a blessing from a priest.

Our group then journeyed to St. Petersburg, where we boarded a ship and set sail for the island of Valaam. Lake Ladoga is the largest freshwater lake in the eastern hemisphere, as our fourteen-hour cruise confirmed. A long slumber on the cruise, accompanied by rich vistas of water and sky, refreshed my body and spirit. As Deacon James shared a few details about the history of Valaam Monastery, the mythical quality given to the place by my imagination swelled.

Two monk-missionaries from the great monasteries of Mt. Athos, off the northern coast of Greece, traveled to the forests of northwestern Russia in the tenth century. Eighty miles east of what is now the border of Finland, Sergius and his follower Herman established Valaam Monastery on the island of Valaam, and the community experienced equal degrees of hardship and prosperity in the centuries that followed. Particularly troublesome were the sixteenth and seventeenth centuries: in 1581, a plague swept Valaam, claiming the lives of thirty-seven monks and forty-seven novices; and in 1611, an invasion of foreign aggressors resulted in severe beatings that killed the abbot and many monks. The monastery was then burned to the ground and remained deserted for over one hundred years. Finally, the Russian emperor Peter the First issued a decree in 1715 to restore Valaam and replenish its monastic population.

The monastery that we would encounter held little evidence of these historical trials. Instead, it was suffering from a fresh wound—seventy-five years of communist persecution. To our eyes, the chapels had decayed and the monks had grieved. But like dandelions through concrete, signs of new life were springing forth.

The fall of the Iron Curtain, when Russia was seeking to improve its global image, caused a fresh wind to blow through the huts and forests of the island. We landed on the shore and received a robust welcome from the abbot. Under the burden of backpacks and language barriers, our group walked the dirt road leading through a short white tunnel into the monastic compound. We passed a few chickens and an old diesel truck. As a cruel accommodation to one of monasticism's ministries, the communist government used the island as a dumping ground for many northern Russians who were poor, handicapped, or mentally ill. These became the fathers and grandfathers of a small population in a nearby village. We passed several of their children on our walk into the courtyard of the monastery.

One of the young boys—sandy-haired and square-jawed— caught my eye. He sat on a high cement block, legs swinging and not at all timid. He was a stocky five-year-old, stuffed into a tight brown sweater. I noticed him because he was the only boy sitting in the midst of six or so male adults. The scene had an air of primitive regality about it, as if the boy were some kind of back-alley king, crowned prematurely in the absence of a long-lost father.

A passing monk told me—without a trace of hyperbole— that this boy was special, for it was widely believed within the Valaam brotherhood that he would one day become the abbot of the monastery. I listened closely, then gazed at the lad. Crouching by the cement block, I drew within a foot or two of the young boy's face. I strained to see if I could discern the nascent virtue. His eyes watched me closely as I made a few funny faces intended to make him laugh. Suddenly, I felt the sharp, localized pain of his small fist upon my cheek! No warning, no explanation . . . no manners! Shocking, I thought. As I walked from the scene, pondering the playful blow I had received from the hand of the tiny abbot-in-training, a verse from the Psalter sprang to mind: "Let the righteous strike me; *it shall be* a kindness" (141:5).

Sufficiently humbled, I joined our group and, after a meal of fish and bread on that first evening, was shuttled by boat to a satellite island where we were to pitch our tents and get an idea of the hard work that lay ahead. Our pilgrimage to Valaam was to include restoration work on the chapel of a monastic skete (a small outpost of the main monastery). We would be carrying rocks and heavy logs from the shore up a winding path through the woods to the worksite. But our pilgrimage was to include a different kind of work, too. We came to put aside—if even for a time—our familiar spiritual customs, those habits softened by years of use in an American culture that consecrates comfort and convenience. And since the Orthodox Church sees no dichotomy between the spiritual and physical, we came to work both our bodies and souls toward salvation.

We were told that we'd be landing at Valaam during the rainy season, but the sky was deep and cloudless and richly blue. Sunset was still a few hours away, which left some time to settle in. I set up my red tent in a small grassy clearing ten feet or so from a tree line. Each supply I brought—clothing, a tool belt, a flashlight, packets of powdered drinks, snacks, a mess kit, an icon or two—was placed in some orderly fashion around the tent or just outside the door. Odd, I thought. When I'm at home, chaos is my decorating scheme. But in such a foreign place with such a foreign purpose, any semblance of order and familiarity seemed crucial to my survival.

"We'll begin work tomorrow," bellowed the deacon to our group, "and take occasional breaks during the week by going to the main island for services." Four or five women, who would prove to have astonishing culinary skills as the month wore on, gathered our first meal. As we gulped our white beans and bread with jam, I wondered at how we gravitate toward those roles with which we are most familiar. No one had asked these women to be the camp cooks, but they leaned into the responsibility in a way that suggested privilege, not burden. I imagined them in their kitchens back home, groping—sometimes lightly, sometimes desperately—for some higher purpose in the everyday mundaneness of preparing meals. My mind drifted through memory: oh yes, I think I know a woman like that.

The island of Valaam rests on the same latitude as Anchorage, Alaska. During the summer months, the sun doesn't cross the sky in a direct line, but in a kind of sharply bent arch. As a result, there is no true darkness to the days of summer, only periods of dimness. Some pilgrims decided to bed down for the night, others to gather kindling for a fire. After conversation with several new friends, I wandered a winding path through the woods to another rocky shore of Lake Ladoga. I surveyed the clear horizon and felt the ancient wind on my face and through my hair. My bare feet covered a small portion of rock that I imagined had supported many holy men through the centuries. I prayed. When my pilgrimage to Valaam Monastery was over, what would be the condition of the man who stood upon it now?

CHAPTER 5

SALVATION AND SWEAT

On the table of my mind were gathered all the references to monasticism I could remember—at least, the ones I encountered before I became an Orthodox Christian. The etchings of stout and satisfied monks; the newspaper cartoons that always had them smiling and saying funny things; the contemporary trend of turning Western-style musical chanting with familiar scales and soothing tones into hit records: all these formed an impression of monastic life as one big cool and breezy sigh, days whiled away by roaming through dandelions in loose, comfortable clothing. There they lie, these references.

I was wrong. Really wrong. Our first day of entering monastic life brought a stern wind that blew that impression clean off the table. Those romanticizations (though not altogether untrue: monks do eat, smile, and make music) are popular because that is what we *want* monasticism to be. Our American culture—including many of us by extension—is unsympathetic to a Christianity that requires, of all things, real effort. Perhaps we are uncomfortable with the idea of a community of Christians somewhere sharing our precepts but shunning our lifestyle. And the idea of community is essential here; one lone eccentric is easy to dismiss, but a collective of believers—unified in behavior and belief—gets our attention.

Monks begin their days early. The sharp clanging of the wake-up bell pierced the walls of my tent around 6:30 A.M. This would be the time and method of waking the troops for our entire stay. Disoriented but determined, I joined the others along a forest path that opened to a scene whose image has since been burned into my soul and shall remain for a lifetime. There, on a cliff hundreds of feet above Lake Ladoga, stood a tall and thick cross. Ten feet in height, made of cement and sweat, this ancient cross was perched like a lighthouse on the edge of the crag.

Birch and aspen trees had been sheared so that the cross could see the world, and the world could see the cross. We gathered here each sunrise for morning prayers, and each sunset to pray the day to a close. This morning's sun wasn't entirely visible behind clouds, but a sienna shade of light rested on the scene. The freshness of this experience—this country, these people, and this adventure—encouraged me to lean harder than usual into our prayers.

Breakfast slid by. Fueled on strange pancakes and jellied bread, our group was divided according to skill and desire. A few young men, hungry for destruction, robustly volunteered to chop wood. Those with stonecutting or bricklaying skills would be assigned to lay the foundation for the cabin we were building. When monks or pilgrims venture to the island for years to come, we want for them a sturdy lodge in which to rest. Several women from our team volunteered to clean the lower of two chapels in the skete. Sixty years of dirt and dust proved to be no match for the loving, determined hands of these laborers.

The weightiest task required transporting logs ranging from

six to twenty feet in length from the dock to the worksite. Before our group arrived, almost two hundred logs had been delivered to the island. A portion of the money we had raised before the pilgrimage helped purchase this wood for the cabin, but the fluctuating value of Russian currency didn't acquire nearly as much as we'd hoped. Still, in keeping with the virtue of contentment, we worked happily with what we had.

One resourceful member of our group fashioned harnesses out of thick sticks and rope cords. By sliding the cord around the log with two workers lifting each end of the stick, eight of us could carry a log from the dock to the worksite. A flat surface or even a gentle downward slope to the path we had to tread would have been lovely, simply lovely. But no. From the dock, the path took a sharp turn to the right and disappeared into a thick, ascending grove of trees. The sharpest incline was reserved for the last thirty yards—a kind of dusty purgatory designed to cleanse the pilgrim of any trace of sloth.

We all worked our respective tasks until the sun was at its highest point. Our cooks rang the bell and skid marks were left in the dirt as we bolted for the firepit. Most of our meals were culled from what the earth at Valaam had to offer: beans, grains, water from the island's well. After lunch, each of us was given a break of an hour or so to do with as we pleased. I wandered back to the rock where I stood barefoot the night we arrived. Kneeling down, I formed a bowl with my hands and brought a taste of Lake Ladoga to my lips. This rock became my resting-place for the pilgrimage. From this southern shore of the island, I could hear no voices.

For so few is the spiritual value of work understood; for fewer still, experienced. We notice in Genesis 2:15 that an original creation mandate was to "tend and keep" the Garden, a mandate given by God in the perfect world before the Fall.

Our example is God Himself. His first appearance in Holy Scripture is in the role of Creator. Because God worked and God is good, work is good. If we become aware, truly aware, of the incredible richness of the natural world around us, we discover that His tasks in creating it were manifold, and the fruit of His labor is "very good."

But Genesis seems immeasurably remote in time, the Garden far away and removed from our experience of work today. One notion that might help shorten the distance is to become reacquainted with the value of manual labor. If we can, for a moment, remove our cultural bias against manual labor as an activity only for the poor or uneducated, we might discover that there is real benefit from working with our hands. Yes, we use our hands to type at a computer or shuffle executive papers, but the creation mandate to "tend and keep" suggests an intensity of effort that removes us from what is comfortable and easy.

Mother Teresa of Calcutta observed that if you want to know what you have done for Jesus at the end of the day, look at your hands. She may have borrowed the idea from St. Paul, who advised the faithful in Thessaloniki to "lead a quiet life, to mind your own business, and to work with your own hands" (1 Thessalonians 4:11). The hands reveal in form and detail what is hiding in the heart. Many of us have settled into lifestyles that insulate us from allowing our hands, our sweat, our creativity to do their part in "working out our salvation" (Philippians 2:12). We can buy our food without planting, our furniture without building, and our fun without creating. For every blessing bestowed upon our world by technology, a curse hides in its shadow.

The creation mandate to "tend and keep" is even more broad in its application than just physical labor. The intensity of effort required of us reaches beyond our gardening and into our relationships. The first time we encounter the principle of "keeping" in the Book of Genesis is in the second chapter, describing how Adam is to take care of the garden in which he is placed. The Hebrew word *shamar* is used here, but its English equivalent—"keep"—is a poor rendering of such a rich concept. Instead, *shamar* suggests a fuller commitment to comprehensive caretaking, a positive condition of loving stewardship. The next time we encounter *shamar* is in Cain's defensive reply, "Am I my brother's keeper?" (Genesis 4:9). We know, of course, that the implicit answer is "yes." Finally, we discover the full and proper description of *shamar* when we face it a third time, now as part of the Aaronic blessing in Numbers 6:24–26:

> The LORD bless you and *keep* you;
> The LORD make His face shine upon you,
> And be gracious to you;
> The LORD lift up His countenance upon you,
> And give you peace.

We are to keep creation, we are to keep each other, as God keeps us. And what is the most powerful symbol of God's keeping of all that He has made? It is the cross. That instrument of death stands as our example of how to live—lovingly, compassionately, sacrificially. Our relationships, then, become wonderful gardens where we perform precious work. To build a friendship, to forgive a loved one, to squeeze our anger silent, to pray away our thirst for revenge, to offer an encouraging word—this is creative labor. When we discover how hard it is to do such work, we recognize that the heart is the first soil to be tended and kept, for from it grows fruit that is bad or good.

Because our physical labor was happening within a monastic context, we pilgrims were encouraged to be sensitive to the value of work beyond the obvious. I noticed, for example, that young monks were often assigned the obedience of labor. After considering how physical labor affected my own disposition, it became clear that work is a good strategy for loosening the grip of carnal appetites. It seemed that one must work the body to control the body. The principle, of course, is lost when we work the body to promote the body, as in any effort to put it on display. But intensity of effort—physical and spiritual—invites a kind of sanity where desire submits to will, and the awareness of our limitations can lead to humility.

The monastic tradition of Christianity offers an experience that unifies strong effort with spiritual intent; it is known, in Russian, as a *podvig*. More than a single deed, it is a condition of the soul. Frivolity, even the instinct of self-preservation, is sacrificed for a time as the soul, mind, and body—burning, aspiring, ascending—engage in a task that focuses on singular dedication to God. The division that we've manufactured between the mysterious and the mundane breaks down, and our vision is trained not to see such a division again.

A *podvig* might be accomplished by the artist who strives to give color and form to his soul's aching for God, without regard for commercial response; it might be performed by the mother who silently cares for her handicapped child, aided only by the relief of her tears; or it might be the work of the priest who, day after day, faithfully offers prayers at his altar in front of an empty temple. Many in Russia believe that a *podvig* comes to a person as his soul is moved by the Holy Spirit in crucial moments of life. It is God who plants, leads; we till the soil of our hearts in preparation to receive.

On our pilgrimage, we encountered men and women for

whom *podvig* was a way of life. Their lifestyles taught us that industry must never replace industriousness. Located in St. Petersburg is a monastic house associated with Valaam, known as a *podvorye*. Once a year, a priest-monk by the name of Father Alexander makes the journey to Valaam for a time of focus and renewal. Having come to our island to observe our work, he shared some of his story with us over tea. His years as a monk have taught him that comfort is an enemy to the monastic life because it anchors the soul to this world. All of us—whether we live within the walls of a monastery or without—must deny the easy life if we are to endeavor for eternal life.

On this trip, Father Alexander, with four monks as companions, made the long journey in seven days. Odd, I thought, since our ship made it in one. He explained that it took seven days for them to row from St. Petersburg, through the Bay of Finland, and up the coast to Valaam. Row? When asked how he got to Valaam, Father Alexander said that he and his men came in a rowboat. They preferred the journey by rowboat because they loved nature. I asked, "Why did you row and not use a motor?" "Because then," he replied, "we could not hear ourselves pray."

Our job was to enter into our log-carrying, our brick-laying, our wood-splitting, our cooking and conversations, with full presence of mind. But so few of us had trained our minds to do anything but feed on distractions. When we resumed our work for the day, the earthy music of Valaam's nature was tainted by the sounds of the very world we were to leave behind. We sang popular songs and whistled the themes to television shows. We chatted about our favorite movies and laughed indiscriminately about their content. We even clouded our mission with references to good things—like family or our favorite foods—all to avoid the deafening awkwardness of silence.

After dinner that evening, a sweet exhaustion lingered. We stumbled past worksites and wheelbarrows and into the chapel we were renovating. Scaffolding had been erected before we arrived, evidence that our work was one strand in a long creative thread. Russian workers and monks from the monastery work on renovating the chapel whenever enough money and supplies are available. It isn't unusual for the work to stop for a year or two, but it is always resumed. We stood in the chapel and took in its musty aroma, its dull wooden walls. The need for renovation, and the evidence of it, was all around. Still, the edifice gave forth an ancient quality suggesting that no polished construct could sufficiently contain its mystery.

This six-hundred-year-old chapel probably had not heard a Vespers service in sixty years. Several icons were placed on a wooden partition in the front of the small nave. It was one of those rare occasions when one didn't mind being in church dressed in soiled clothing and without having recently bathed. A priest from our group offered incense as the service began, but none of us took that personally. We felt incredibly happy to be present, at home in a place we'd never been. The hymns, the psalms, the petitions of the service supported the collective weight of our feeble attempts in offering them. Dirty pilgrims, tired hands, thankful hearts.

At the end of the day, a few pilgrims gathered at the cross on the cliff to drink deeply the wide vista of Lake Ladoga and to swap stories. Holding my left hand in my right, I noticed a small blister developing on the fleshy fold where my fingers met my palm. I wasn't paying particular attention to anything. The breeze carried this tired mind along the day's events, along the island paths that had absorbed the dirt and sweat mixture that had fallen from our faces. There it lay in the ground, mingled with the dirt and sweat of other men from other centuries, some of whom erected this cross whose lengthening shadow falls behind. I lifted my face toward the great water and closed my eyes, remembering: We can work for treasure that fades, or for treasure hidden in a place where rust and moth do not destroy.

CHAPTER 6

THE RHYTHM OF VIGILANCE, THE PULSE OF PRAYER

The example of Father Alexander and his tenacious crewmen yields an insight into one of monasticism's fundamental truths—vigilance is an all day, every day affair. We Christians are to be a watchful people. In the prayers of preparation to be recited before receiving Holy Communion, we ask God to draw us near to Him, lest we "stray and become prey of the wolf of souls." Really, the devil doesn't deserve such good poetry. But the image is powerful—the beast is always near, seeking whom he may devour. The monk confesses that he cannot save himself, that it is God and God alone who does the saving. But, as C. S. Lewis has written, God "cannot ravish. He can only woo." [3] Our response to God's initiative, like the monk's, is crucial. Our real job, then, is to answer "yes."

We pilgrims learned quickly that monks go to church, often. They work the body by labor and the soul by prayer. Although prayer was to be poured into all the day's activities—digging, eating, playing, even sleeping—we discovered the church to be the center of monastic life. The Orthodox Church believes that revelation is found in the Church. What is revealed? The priest intones the answer at the beginning of the

55

Divine Liturgy—that there is a Kingdom, that it is blessed, and that it is of the Father, the Son, and the Holy Spirit. Monastics are to live in constant remembrance of that; indeed, they rarely get a chance to forget.

The monastic rule is what keeps the monk aware. By it, the monk is safeguarded in his daily activity to keep vigil on his inward condition. The monastery as a whole observes a rule of life and prayer laid down by its founders. In addition, a monk's personal rule is the order of life that is prescribed to him by his abbot or his spiritual father, often taking into consideration the specific needs of his past, his present, and his future. It includes both a personal prayer rule and a set of tasks for each day, called "obediences." While we pilgrims worked and walked the grounds at Valaam, we observed a lot of motion. Some monks fulfilled their obediences by caring for those in the infirmary, others by painting icons or shuffling music papers in preparation for an upcoming service. Several could be seen carrying shovels while another stitched a robe or two. Though their obediences were different, all were to be kept unfailingly. And that was the secret to the rule's power of protection—it must be faithfully kept.

Attending church services is what every monk's rule had in common. Services were held periodically throughout the day and night at Valaam, so every monk had an opportunity to attend. The main Valaam church has two naves, only one of which was in use. The main nave was then but a shadow of its past glory. For many years the cold hands of a collapsed Russian economy had chipped away at the stone and paint of the cavernous room. When we arrived, scaffolding had been erected and huge plastic tarps hung from the ceiling to protect the icons during protracted efforts of renovation. As our eyes took it all in, we felt the balance between a monastic spirituality committed to simplicity and an artistic expression devoted to divinity. Great art, great architecture, always leads us inward and upward.

Valaam's main church has another nave—a long, concrete rectangle of a room that will hold all the services until the main nave is restored. Far from being just a "this-will-have-to-do" alternative, the worship space contains some of Valaam's great treasures—the relics of St. Sergius and St. Herman, the two missionaries who founded the monastery in the tenth century; a chip of the rock on which St. Seraphim of Sarov, a great nineteenth-century Russian saint, prayed for a thousand consecutive days; and a large, ancient icon of the Theotokos, or Mary, the Mother of God. These are more than tourist attractions; they are genuine sacred objects worthy of veneration.

This lower nave housed a remarkable drama one evening as many of us witnessed two novices being tonsured to become monks. Tonsuring is an initiation ritual that includes cutting tiny fragments of hair from four corners—in the shape of a cross—from the head. The hair is then burned in a candle flame as a symbol that all we have to offer God is ourselves, our very being. A liturgical expression of profound humility and personal decision, the service unfolds and the lessons flow forth.

In the darkened nave, illumined only by candles, a long red carpet is stretched from the marble tomb of Ss. Sergius and Herman to near the front of the altar—a distance of twenty yards or so. The two novices lay their bodies down, with faces on the floor and arms spread to the side. Lining both sides of the carpet are monks dressed in black, each facing in and holding a finger-and-thumb's worth of the monks' robes on his right and left in fence-like fashion, chanting an astonishing melody. That song! Deep voices and old Slavonic language—mysterious utterances that penetrate the bodies and souls of us illiterate listeners.

As the monks chant and move slowly toward the altar, the two novices inch their bodies forward on the carpet using only their hands and arms. Their faces stay down. Every five yards they stop and the abbot, who is standing near the altar, intones his part. This gradual procession is more than a symbol of respect; it is humility itself. The novices reveal our true condition when we as humans buckle beneath the burden of our sins. God draws us toward Him, and we do not strut, but crawl.

Finally, the novices reach the abbot. The abbot is holding the scissors to be used to tonsure the two into the monastic brotherhood. As the novices stand and face the abbot, we suddenly hear the sharp metallic jangle of scissors hitting the cement floor. The abbot has tossed them purposefully to the ground in front of one of the novices. The novice bends, picks them up, and hands them back to the abbot. It happens again—the jangle, the bend, the return. And a third time! Each novice participates in this three-part dance. The significance? No one forces the novice to pick up the scissors. A very personal decision to follow God is being made, and made voluntarily, as an act of the will.

That all this activity is happening just to the left of the large icon of the Theotokos—literally, the "Birthgiver of God"—is noteworthy, I think. The purest expression of willing cooperation is to be found in her. The account in the first chapter of St. Luke reveals Mary to be a thoughtful, by no means naive, recipient of Gabriel's annunciation. Mary was "greatly troubled at his words," and we can almost see the furrowed brow on her forehead when she wonders aloud, "How can this be since I am a virgin?" Then, she concurs immediately, willingly, simply. She is a model of submission for all: she did that which gives the monk, the layperson, the whole world an example of obedience; she responded with that simple but powerful act that brought heaven to earth; she said, "Let it be to me according to your word"; in short, Mary answered "Yes!"

As the days passed during our Valaam pilgrimage, our group slowly sensed that monastic life isn't here to impress, but to challenge. The monastic strives to say "yes" to God in every decision, in all places, at all times. Attending church services here in the lower nave is a significant part of learning how to say "yes" more frequently and less grudgingly. Some come to the services with joyful anticipation, some just wanting the roof to cave in, but they all come knowing that the steady recitation of the psalms, the constant prayers, the long readings from Scripture, all of these work on a person. The fact is that we're all here with hard hearts. But our group was challenged to attend services faithfully: a steady drop of water will crack a stone, but throwing a bucketful once a month does no good.

The job for some monks was to be in the temple most of the day. At Valaam, as in every Orthodox monastery, the devotional rhythm of every day flows from the Prophet David's words in Psalm 119:164: "Seven times a day I praise You, / Because of Your righteous judgments." We were occasionally reminded that as we were working on the island, the church was humming. The enormous bell that calls the monks to prayer could be heard every few hours. And every monk entered the church to discover—again and again—who he was and to whom he belonged.

Each of the seven services has a name—Vespers; Compline;

the Midnight Office; Matins; First Hour; Third Hour; Sixth Hour; Ninth Hour. There is a deliberate flow to the services as they visit the stages of the life of Christ, the Apostles, and the Church. To observe this Christian day is to invite divine mystery into the ordinary day; it is to use time to step outside of time. Fresh from home, and novices in our observance, we pilgrims felt a division between our lives inside the church and our lives outside that was clear and defined. But as the weeks flowed, the distinctions were getting wonderfully hazy, not so abrupt and obvious.

As the services unfold, the monk is reminded of his great and personal need for so glorious a salvation, for he learns of man's fall into sin and of his expulsion from paradise. The Vespers service is ultimately a service of thanksgiving, and specific psalms are read—such as Psalm 104, that glorious litany of God's wonders in creation—that render the monk mindful of God's hand of salvation upon His people.

Vespers leads into the Compline service, which derives its name from the Latin term *completorium*, meaning "complement." Here, the monk prays that the coming night may be free from corrupting fantasy. This and other services contain sections that remain identical from day to day, but also use prayers and canons and hymns that change daily and that celebrate a saint or historical event.

The monk enters into the service of the Midnight Office at or shortly after midnight, and he is reminded of great unknowing. Night is a time for vigilance: Christ proclaims that He will "come as a thief in the night" and that "no man knows the day nor the hour wherein the Son of man comes." This service might last until three in the morning. Immediately following is Matins, carrying the monk until dawn. All Orthodox church altars are to face the east, toward the rising sun. Light is born at dawn, and salvation is near.

The First Hour, which immediately follows Matins, leads the monk to a condition of thankfulness. As he stifles every yawn, he is reminded by the psalm that God's mercies are new this morning, every morning. Or, maybe, that he has a new opportunity to experience them, to allow them to change the way he interacts with his neighbor. The hymns he sings welcome this new Light as the Light that is the same yesterday, today, and forever. The First Hour, with its references to renewal, reminds the monk that morning is not so much a time of day as it is a glimpse into timelessness. All of creation near to him is still, and anticipating. The dove, the frog, the crow— they awaken into a state of dependence. The former Trappist monk Thomas Merton observed that these animals "speak to God, not with fluent song, but with an awakening question that is their dawn state . . . they ask if it is time for them to 'be.'" Divine permission is given, and the morning song builds from a chirp to a choir.

The activities in and around the monastery are underway now. The Third Hour carries the monk to that time when those early conspirators planned the death of our Lord. Additionally, the hymnody of this hour recounts the descent of the Holy Spirit on the Day of Pentecost. The Sixth Hour commemorates the Passion and Crucifixion of Christ. Many psalms are read during these services and in the periods in between. Intertwining psalms throughout his day, the monk learns the many ways they are alive. He does not dwell on them; they dwell on him.

With the Ninth Hour comes a reflection of when and why the Lord laid down His life for the life of the world. The hymns and prayers are sober now. But the edges of every monastic service are colored with the reality of the Resurrection. Sadness lingers, but does not win. Nearing His Crucifixion, Christ told His disciples that, yes, "you will be sorrowful, but your sorrow will be turned into joy" (John 16:20). When Vespers arrives, the monk is reminded just how universal and permeating is creation's joy. Psalm 104 is chanted, and he sees that every fiber, every detail of creation flows from God's plan and toward God's purpose:

> O Lord my God, Thou art very great;
> Thou art clothed with splendor and majesty.
> He wraps Himself in light as with a garment;
> He stretches out the heavens like a tent
> And lays the beams of His upper chambers
>   on their waters . . .
> He set the earth on its foundations;
> It can never be moved . . .
> O Lord, how manifold are Thy works!
> In wisdom hast Thou made them all.

Finally, the after-supper prayer brings the monk back to that condition from where he started his day—thankfulness. For having awakened; for the limbs of his body that have carried him; for the clarity of his mind available to have thought on things above; for having worked with his hands at tasks mundane at the surface, but pregnant with meaning; for having felt the tall grass under his feet; for having kissed the hand of his priest; for all the breaths and for all the beats of his heart, the monk strives to be thankful. But there is more. Confronting his own brokenness, the monk discovers the value of his spiritual poverty. Perhaps the remembrance of a harsh word spoken by him to a brother pulled his conscience toward repentance; perhaps the lazy or careless handling of his chores has reaped a needed correction from his abbot; or maybe the quiet anger that he cannot explain keeps him humble and open to mercy. The monk is thankful not for his sin, but for the way his gracious God uses even his weaknesses and failures to instruct.

Toward the end of the last service of the day, the monk hears about death. Still, for this confrontation he is thankful. If temptation reminds the monk to be vigilant, death requires it. Reflecting upon his mortality supports a clear and firm adjustment of his priorities. It is a reflection that leads not to self-absorption, but to self-denial. Sin drains life; and life is too precious and full of beauty to waste. In monastic history, it is not unusual for monks to build their own coffins and keep them near their cells. When motivation toward virtue is running thin, a glance toward that thin wooden carton may make all the difference.

Like a magnet, the services of the Church keep pulling the monk back to what is important. They remind him what all the work is for. He hears about eternal life, about that other Kingdom that requires participation on his part if he is to be a citizen. Citizenship in that Kingdom is a gift from God, but gifts have to be received. He, like us, must learn how to empty his hands of everything he uses as substitutes.

Occasionally, when I'm feeling fussy and barely willing to surrender another minute of my Sunday morning to church, I remember those services at Valaam. Surely those monks have struggled, at some time, with *why* they attend and *why* the maturity for which they seek so often eludes them. But at least the presence of struggle is the evidence of effort. Monastics teach us how to pray for the present grace to fight the present temptation in the present hour. And don't waste any more time, they say. "Be vigilant, for it is later than you think."

CHAPTER 7

MONK FOR A DAY

If we followed westward winds from the monastery, crossing Lake Ladoga and a thread of land that holds the border of Russia and Finland, we would find the Gulf of Finland resting there. Farther west still is the bigger Gulf of Bothnia, separating Finland from Sweden. These two gulfs meet and pour their union into the northern tip of the Baltic Sea. On a colorful map, the gulfs and the sea form a big blue lobster, with the left claw much larger than the right. Its body rubs the coasts of Latvia, Poland, and Germany, reaches into the North Sea, then finally is laid to rest in the Atlantic Ocean.

Two gulfs, one sea. The image came to mind when a powerful truth was presented to me by the abbot. He allowed several of us pilgrims to leave behind our work on the satellite island and spend a full twenty-four hours on the main island. Permission was granted to be a "monk for a day." And a day was just about as long as I could handle ("so *this* is what it means to 'work out your salvation with fear and trembling'!"). But under the heavy mantle of physical labor and church service attendance, that powerful truth emerged—if not learned, if not understood, at least observed: work and prayer are two inseparable currents that carry us toward maturity.

65

Not many years before my Valaam pilgrimage, I considered maturity a dubious destination. But even the briefest stroll through the carnage of adolescence—where bravado, impulsiveness, and individualism run roughshod over mind, body, and soul—prompts one to consider the alternative of growing up. Of course, maturity does not exempt one from vice; our heroes and our elders are quite imperfect. But what hit me with greater force wasn't that work and prayer help us grow; it was rather that, in the Christian view of mystery, work and prayer—the physical and the spiritual—are inseparable.

I left the island late in the evening. The motorized skiff slid across the water quietly, unobtrusively. There were three of us in the boat, and we exchanged only enough conversation to fill half a page. I played a personal game of closing one eye to see how much of the forest in the background I could obscure by focusing on the large trees in the foreground, the ones closest to the shoreline. Other than the gruff and husky pilot of our boat, no wildlife was visible. But those great trees, that dark water, and that clean air were deeply satisfying. The hum of the motor did nothing to diminish my appreciation for that plot of earth. I caught myself in a momentary condition that was—at last—close to pure monastic contemplation: *The earth is the Lord's and the fullness thereof; blessed be the name of the Lord.* And as quickly as I became conscious of purely contemplating, I just as quickly lost it.

We arrived at the main monastery and shared a pot of tea with an English-speaking priest-monk, or "hieromonk." After his explanation of monastic life, we received advice on how to be—or, rather, *whom* to be—during our stay at the main island. "Be yourself," I felt him saying, "no one else is as qualified." And that meant that we had to prepare for the Sacrament of Confession.

Preparing to confess is almost as important as the confession itself. When confronted with the sobering question, "What have you done with My image within you?" one might feel like a proud child who eagerly raises his hand because he thinks he has the right answer, or like a shamed child who shoves his hands in his pockets, looks to the ground, and kicks a few stones.

I usually feel like hiding. But when we hear that question, it is in the preparation—the thoughtful, prayerful reflection that yields our most honest and penetrating responses—that we discover much of who we are and much of who God is.

Much, not all. The Prophet Jeremiah reminds us that "[our] heart is . . . desperately wicked; / Who can know it?" (17:9) and Isaiah affirms that "as the heavens are higher than the earth, / So are My ways higher than your ways, / And My thoughts than your thoughts" (55:9). That mystery of unknowing, then, invites humility. A penetrating preparation for confession reminds us that our need is infinitely greater than we know for a God who is infinitely greater than we can comprehend.

Our visit with the hieromonk lasted an hour or so. Fresh from his advice, I found a spot on the cement stairs outside his room and began my inventory. So, over the course of my life, what had I done with God's image within me? Hmm, I see. More tea, please.

After we three pilgrims caught ninety minutes of sleep on wooden cots with thin blankets, a monk's gentle knock still managed to rattle the door. At least he tried to be merciful. We poured our socked feet into our boots and ambled the half-mile path toward the church. The sky was not dark, just dim; the breeze, not cool but cold. The first order of the day— coming at a brisk three A.M.—was to attend the morning service that would last until dawn. St. Basil the Great considered Psalm 63 to be a perfect morning prayer:

> O God, Thou art my God,
> Early shall I seek Thee.
> My soul thirsts for Thee,
> My flesh longs for Thee
> In a dry and thirsty land
> Where there is no water.
> So I have looked for Thee in the sanctuary
> To see Thy power and Thy glory.
> Thy lovingkindness is better than life;
> So shall my lips praise Thee.
> I shall praise Thee as long as I live,
> And in Thy name shall I lift up my hands . . .
> On my bed I shall remember Thee,
> And I shall meditate on Thee in the night watches.
> Because Thou art my help,
> I shall sing in the shadow of Thy wings.
> I shall stay close to Thee,
> For Thy right hand upholds me . . .

My body and soul began to warm as I entered the nave, lit a candle, and venerated the many icons. The service allows for some movement. An Orthodox church service is itself an icon of the relationship between earth and heaven, where we move around the "world" inside the temple, engaged in subtle activities charged with meaning, while prayers are being offered "for all and in behalf of all." The Orthodox Church helped restore for me the sacredness of place. Over time, over the course of attending the services, I have come more and more to rely on the sure and sane simplicity of Psalm 63: God is

God; I long for Him; He can be found in the sanctuary.

But moments of this kind of clarity are still just moments. I stumbled around the nave and found my place to stand. Most of the service I spent by adding up the distractions and figuring that they amounted to a colossal waste of my time. Yes, I wanted to "enter in" to the worship experience, but how about at a reasonable hour and after a hearty breakfast? And all this standing is hard on the knees. Like a prodigal son, my mind wandered far from the altar and indulged in everything but worship. But prodigality, as the parable suggests, can lead to a recognition of need—"but when he came to himself" (Luke 15:17)—that, in turn, brings us back home. There in the early hours at Valaam, the Father was taking me back again and again and again.

When the First Hour services came to a close, a collection of us moved next door for a meal. It is customary for Americans to chat over food; we gather, we eat, we talk. But in the monastery, mealtime is no less a time of vigilance than nighttime. Instead of conversation, we listened to a novice fulfill his monastic obedience by reading in the strong consonant Russian language from the Psalms or from a book about the lives of the saints. Our meal was peppered with occasional rings from the abbot's hand bell, which indicated his decision to move on to the next course. We could utter a brief request— "please pass the potatoes"—but our mouths were to do one thing at a time, and this time we were to be eating.

Monasticism is often caricatured as joyless. In *The Name of the Rose,* a mystery novel set within a monastic community, author Umberto Eco draws a character who emphatically teaches that laughter is a sin. Eco's grumpy monk lurks in the shadows and halls of the monastery, poised to chasten any brother who might be having something resembling a good time. My experience at Valaam was such that a monk like that would be out of place. There were times—after the meals, for example—when I was refreshed by the low sound of men laughing. And it was never cleverness or a sophisticated joke, but often simple things that provoked a sweet response: a monk's beard brushing his salad, an awkward language impasse, a muffled burp.

Standing beside these men only during the services painted an unbalanced portrait of their personalities, for they did other things than just attend church. While I had the privilege to be a "monk for a day," I accompanied them as they struggled to walk that delicate balance that joins the physical and the spiritual. Prayer was never *just* prayer, and work was never *just* work. To worship in the church required the physical discipline of an athlete; to dig a ditch required the spiritual focus of, well, a monk. Engage the body, engage the mind, engage the soul in constant awareness of God. To be fully alive is to be fully aware. There they were, those lesson-givers, offering clues on how to wake up and live.

After our meal, I walked a couple of miles with three monks to a patch of island that held several large sand dunes. Our task for the next several hours was to shovel sand into a waiting truck. I didn't know how the sand was to be used; I just knew that, because of the thick wall of language incompatibility, I should do what they did. So I shoveled.

The vast blue sky gripped a blazing sun and seemed to slow it down so it could bake our bodies till we were tender. I shed a thick wool shirt, but, in deference to modesty over comfort, kept wearing a sleeveless T-shirt instead of stripping to the waist altogether. My monkish brethren shoveled in their cassocks, ignoring the dusty film that clung to the sweat-soaked fabric of those long robes. And their lips moved in silent speech as they flung sand. I assumed they were praying; or cursing, I suppose, for the conditions were miserable. Later that day, an interpreter told me that they were probably "practicing the presence of God." Practicing? How does one practice a presence?

First, by seeing what is there: sand, a shovel, a truck. Then, by transforming the task at hand: to the monk, those big dunes of sand resemble the sin that weighs him down; that shovel reminds him of the tools given him by the Church—prayer, fasting, confession, service—that allow for that sand to be removed, bit by bit; and that truck, the one that removes the sand, is like the Cross of Christ that removes the sin forever. And finally, one practices by doing what needs to be done: picking up the shovel, scooping the sand, loading the truck; picking up, scooping, loading. In small, steady increments, the monks transformed the mundane into the mysterious, and the mysterious into the mundane.

Instead of joining them on this beautiful spiritualization, I remained emphatically carnal. It was hot and I was desperately thirsty. Disgruntled, too. At least the church was encased in cool concrete. Perhaps we should go back there to, uh, "reflect," at least until the sun goes down. Or even seek shade from the tall bushes that line the shore. Shore? Of course, there's a shore down there! And where there is a shore, there is water!

As the monks worked ceaselessly, I periodically wandered to the water's edge and scooped handfuls of that sweet nectar. Surveying the inlet and savoring the drink, I imagined this lake to be fed by a tributary straight from the Garden of Eden. The water, though, wasn't as clear as I thought it would be. Shell hash and sand stirred together must have created the cloudiness. But to a tired and thirsty pilgrim, it was more than sufficient.

We shoveled for what felt like not a day shy of seventy years. Then, as if obeying some internal timepiece, the monks simply stopped shoveling. We had no blowing horn to indicate the end of our shift, but later I found that we had worked for five hours. Two truckloads of sand were apparently enough to satisfy the current need. Sweaty and disoriented, I lumbered with the monks back to the main temple for another round of services.

This time, though, something would be different. After shaking the sand from my boots, I entered the temple and found my spot on which I had become accustomed to stand. My fatigue surrendered to the soothing aesthetics of the incense aroma, the comforting icons, and the sweet glow of beeswax candle flames. But drinking deeply from the props was not unusual, for the thick language barrier prevented me from understanding the script anyway. No, what was unusual was that, at last—after days of observing these monks and their way of life, which up until now I'd only read about, after feeling alienated from communal worship because of an incomprehensible language, after being confronted so often with the painful difference between who I was and who I wanted to be—at last, I entered in.

Every element converged into a fleeting but finally understandable whole. I heard the precious music that rings from every pure exchange between the physical and the spiritual, that place where God takes compassion on His own and offers a bit of Himself. To be fully present was imperative; all of me, all my fatigue, all the struggle, doubt, joy, and all my past was laid there on the cool concrete floor. I swept past the language barrier and, even if briefly, into a sane world of simple peace, a peace that passes all understanding.

The English-speaking hieromonk stood waiting. He was

wearing a special stole, the sign of a priest who is ready to hear confessions. I reached into my back pocket for a dusty and sandy piece of folded notebook paper, the one that held my broad inventory of when and where I had been an image-maker, an image-breaker. Holding my life in both hands, I approached the hieromonk. Standing to his right, before an icon of Christ, I unfolded the paper and waited for his cue. He lifted his stole and placed it gently over my hunched shoulders and nodded his head. I began to read softly.

The hieromonk and I went on our own pilgrimage through the once-forgotten land of my past. My inventory of where I had sinned and fallen short of the glory of God served as narration. In the comforting womb of Valaam's temple, we visited the home of my youth and the dark spaces of my family; traveled through high school and college and through the years of adolescent discovery and frustration; journeyed through the directionless post-college wasteland where lessons are learned only in hindsight and stained around the edges with regret.

Standing motionless, we wandered the secret airless places. And at the end of that dark inventory, the one that included every moment and experience I could remember when I had chosen unwisely, I stood silent again. The hieromonk leaned closely toward my ear and in an English shaded with Russian accent he offered this: "It is good that you have come to Valaam. Leave your burden here, and from now on learn to love God above all. Go with the assurance that you are forgiven."

No sermon was necessary; the Sacrament of Confession had done its work. The stole was removed from my shoulders as I bent to kiss the icon of Christ, before whom I had confessed. As I returned to my standing place, I took special notice of my legs. They felt light and strong. I seemed to carry my frame with an ease I'd not experienced before. My movements were quick and efficient. As I raised my face and saw the expanse of the temple, the colors came toward me in sharper contrast, the candle flames shone with brighter strength. Even then, I knew that this was a moment's clarity: "To the pure all things are pure" (Titus 1:15). Yes, I will take this moment for as long as it lasts and preserve it in my heart. When the world falls dark again because I have chosen unwisely, I will remember this time. And, like Tennyson's Ulysses, I shall be "strong in will; to strive, to seek, to find, and not to yield."[4]

Housing a confluence of matter and spirit, that church became for me everything that was true and right and possible. God created the world, and the world is good! In His design, all the elements of the earth serve His purposes—wood and dye become icons, beeswax becomes a candle, thread and fabric clothe these monks and villagers, culled and dried sap becomes incense, dirt and cement become floor and pillar. And most importantly, flesh and bone receive the breath of life and become these strange people standing beside me. The Incarnation has sent a glorious shock wave through everything that is and will be. And it is good. It is very good!

The minutes drifted by unnoticed. The closing of the service came just as the monks grew restless and several emerged from the altar area. Drinking deeply from the moment, I lingered until I was one of the last in the church. I knew I would not see this place again in the same way, with the same eyes. I turned to cross the long and wide floor toward the door. Yes, I remember from my years of searching for answers outside the Orthodox Church that experiences like this are, for me, fleeting and rare. They don't come just when I feel I need them most; they simply come when I need them. "When the student is ready, the teacher will appear."

7 · MONK FOR A DAY

As the cool night air gently burned my nose and lungs and the dark sky hung cloudless, I walked the dirt road with my fellow pilgrims to the waiting boat. The Native Americans have their liturgical context and the Zen Buddhists have theirs. Tonight, I have mine. I am here at Valaam so that I will never again mistake the varying degrees of shade for the Light Itself.

St. John Chrysostom, the fourth-century bishop of Antioch, points the way for this pilgrim:

> Never separate yourself from the Church. For nothing is stronger than the Church. Your hope is in the Church alone; your salvation is inside the Church only, your refuge is the Church. She is higher than the heavens, and wider than the whole earth. She never grows old, but is always full of vigor and vitality. Holy Scripture (which would not even exist were it not for the Church), when pointing to Her strength and stability, calls her an unshakable mountain.[5]

CHAPTER 8

"DON'T JUST DO SOMETHING, STAND THERE!"

What I knew of monks before I arrived at Valaam was that they prayed and they worked. Indeed, with even a cursory glance at monastic literature one might detect a faint aroma of incense and sweat floating from the page. What is not as publicized is the critical role that rest and play assume in the life of a monastery. A monk who ignores the Sabbath refreshment of God is soundly in danger of working himself to death.

The path that stretched from the dock, through the forest, into the opening, and past the firepit ended uncleanly in a patch of thick brushweed not far from a *banya*—a small sauna. The grass there was as thick as the path was worn. A pilgrim would average a dozen trips a day along the path while executing his chores. Not so frequent, but usually more gratifying, were the spirited jogs beyond the smooth dirt and into that brushweed where, in twenty yards or so, the *banya* stood waiting. After a few days of monastic flex and strain, the gentle heat and moisture of an hour in the *banya* was delicious.

The old wooden construct contained a small changing room just inside the outer door, another door into a sweat room, a few benches, and an open-faced stove. The whole edifice couldn't have covered more than twenty square feet. Scattered near the mouth of the *banya* were bare, brittle skeletons of birch branches—the tools of *banya* occupants from a previous age. Birch branches with full leaves were slapped against bare skin, causing the pores to open and sweat. Physical impurities of all kinds would leave the body.

When I returned to our skete after the long day of work and prayer, I possessed just enough energy to slide into the water near the dock. Although our pilgrimage was happening in late summer, Lake Ladoga is far enough north never to let bare skin enter without a cold shock. I had been in chilly water before, but this was a new experience! Unable to manage more than a few minutes in this liquid snow, I emerged with fresh determination to find the *banya*. I did find it, and had it not been for the pesky obligations of life in the outside world, I might have remained in that warm sauna until I withered into oblivion.

The ecosystem around the *banya,* on the skete, and surrounding the entire monastery is wild and beautiful. As I entered into Valaam work and prayer, I had only to raise my eyes in any direction to behold a rich, refreshing world. That the ascetic labor here unfolds in this environment adds to it a sense of reassurance, as if the peace and purity for which the laborers are striving are near and visible. Our pilgrims took delight in the island's cliffs and slopes and straits. Resting long enough to enjoy God's creation is as important as recognizing His six days of creative effort.

As strict adherents to the commandments of God, these monastics search for ways to honor the Sabbath principle of rest in their weekly rhythm. They believe that the Bible not only allows, but requires that a period of rest be set aside for people, for animals, and for the land. Rest was designed by

God to protect humanity from perpetual labor, to help us pull our lives together again. Also, rest is needed by the nonhuman life cycle here; every stretch of farmed land needs a break from its productivity precisely so that it can continue being productive.

As I ambled around the island and observed the monks in their various obediences, I was struck by something: monks move slowly. I refer not necessarily to their walking stride, but to some greater, even subtler form of being. There was at Valaam a theology of movement. Tasks that would have been promptly dispatched by an industrious work ethic—like building things or moving piles—were undertaken with a casual tone. And to that same industrious work ethic, monks might appear hopelessly lazy. I knew them not to be lazy, so I tried to reconcile their unhurried physicality with their intense spirituality. Most monks work hard, just slowly. I sensed, then, that there is here a deep appreciation of time.

I am reminded of that old expression: Stop and smell the roses. The formula is meaningless if it is stripped of either its appeal to slowness or its disclosure of the benefits that slowing down will bring. The fragrant bloom of a rose is difficult to sniff when one is sprinting past it. We rest in order to appreciate.

From Valaam we can learn the sanity of frequent prayer, the sobriety of physical labor, and the benefit of periodic rest. Henry David Thoreau asked, "Why should we live with such hurry and waste of life?"[6] It's a good question, and one pointed straight toward my heart as it thumps frantically from the latest exertion. We who are members of a fast society need the example of monasticism to remind us of what we may be missing. And what we are missing may be personal and unique to each of us, like some golden thread to our lives that lies buried and invisible.

One friend found her golden thread on this pilgrimage to Valaam. It was balance, and she knew it had been missing from her life for as long as she had been involved in social work. She came to Valaam fresh from another pilgrimage, one that carried her from the ravages of an addiction to alcohol through a twelve-step program designed to return her life to her. Helping to restore a monastery was a perfect way to keep those idle hands busy, and to undergo restoration herself.

Her disposition tended toward the active and the practical, like that of most social workers. And toward the pragmatic—doing what needed to be done by any means necessary. She moved through the chapels and services and tourist stations with deliberateness, revealing some of the force she kept handy to secure justice for others. In her face I saw no trace of levity, only a few wrinkles in places that suggested she experienced life with the solemnity of a stoic. She laughed, but not easily nor often.

One afternoon, I and several others stood in her company as she served questions to a Valaam monk about the monastery's charity toward the small village nearby. The village was populated by men, women, and children who survived almost exclusively on the food given to them by the monks. My friend saw this ministry as crucial to the monastery's reasons for being, and her gentle interrogation seemed designed as much to affirm as to investigate.

Harder for her to accept, though, was the ostensible languor—that slowness of being—that weighed upon the pace of life in the monastery. She had promptly identified both the problem and the measures needed to resolve it. To her audience of one monk and an interpreter, she explained the horror of poverty, the shame of hunger, the advantage of good agriculture, the inspiration of employment, and the necessity to turn these poor villagers into a self-sustaining proud republic. With polite deference toward the monk, she graciously asked if the monastery could do more to help. Dramatizing her question, she poked the air with her finger toward several groups of monks who appeared to be relaxing. Taken as a whole—language and gesture and subtext—her message seemed to be: Don't just stand there, do something!

To all of this the monk listened. He expressed through the interpreter that the monastery is helping the village with all things necessary for survival. But he also explained that the monks live a life of poverty also, and that poverty and humility are qualities of a monk's life for the rest of his days. With great gentleness he suggested that we Americans have traveled to Valaam to help only for a season, while the monks at Valaam help others for a lifetime. One must keep a balance—one must not always work or serve, but must take time to be refreshed and to experience joy. One must rest from labor as God rested from His labor on the Sabbath. We must learn to dance even as the bombs of hell fall around us. Taken as a whole—language and graciousness and wisdom—his response seemed to be: Don't just do something, stand there.

This was instructive to all of us. We listened to the monk and were reminded that even devotion to good works is idolatry if it interferes with our devotion to Christ, whose own life seemed to strike a balance between mission and reflection, between work and rest. To labor incessantly for a better world may be a subtle expression of pride, as if we could fashion the world in our image while cherishing our indispensable role in doing so. The Psalmist says, "Unless the LORD builds the house, / They labor in vain who build it" (127:1). With an imagination redeemed by Christ, we may be able to envision a world much different from the one in which we currently live. But

Christ remains the Fashioner, we are His workers; we are to worship the Light instead of anything that can be seen because of the Light.

So I witnessed monastic life and was encouraged to pay attention to the speed at which I lived my own life—in a word, to practice mindfulness. I came to Valaam with an American's enthusiasm for productivity, and from an existence that valued stress and pressure as indications that though I might not be doing anything of value, at least I was doing something. But mindfulness is different. It is the quality of life suggested in Christ's Sermon on the Mount—that we choose daily the blessed way of the Gospel; that we keep a close watch on the condition of our hearts; that we pray as we have been taught; and that we live life one day at a time and give no worry for tomorrow. To be mindful is to be aware, and to be aware is to be fully alive.

In biblical Hebrew, a root word exists that suggests a freedom and security that come with space and with the shedding of constrictions. Using the letters *yodh* and *shin,* other words are formed—*yesha* and *yeshua,* for example—that refer to the salvation of all things. We notice here that space and salvation are related, but we don't need a Hebrew lexicon to understand why sacred space is important to a life of wholeness and balance. Instead, I think most of us feel our need for sacred space intuitively.

When I was a child, I was drawn to the passages of Scripture that featured the grand and jarring activity of Christ, the kind of activity that would have grabbed first-century newspaper headlines. That cleansing temples and calming storms was the preference of a child's imagination is not surprising, of course. Less compelling were the quieter times when Christ would retreat to the hills to pray in solitude. But as I matured

82

and felt the need to develop my own relationship with still-ness, those passages of quiet reflection and solitary prayer be-came more important to me. God rested; so should I.

Monks and nuns don't get everything right; they meet temptation and fall into sin as humans often do. And their periods of rest are sometimes indulgences in sloth. But as I moved through my pilgrimage at Valaam, the slowness of be-ing seemed mostly purposeful, appropriate, even earned. It was as if the monks devoted the same mindfulness to rest as they devoted to work, to prayer, and to the hundred small routines required of any person who simply lives.

When I received the blessing, and the burden, to go to the main island to practice the monastic life for a full day, I was grieved to discover that my day began a few hours after mid-night. The long service was followed at dawn by a bad meal and a long walk to the sand pits. There, I worked for hours in the hot sun, and the hot sun worked for hours on me. Brief sips of Lake Ladoga were my only reprieve. Still, though these conditions were brutal, I was not to allow them to disturb the interior peace that at least made them bearable. A terrible soul will erode the foundation of a man faster than a terrible cir-cumstance: Job was righteous in adversity, and found favor; his friends were rife with treachery even as disengaged specta-tors, and fell away.

A mysterious relationship exists between soul and cir-cumstance. To speak of ecology is to speak of connections, relations, intimacies. It is to consider an organism not in isola-tion, but in relationship to its surroundings. To see the cos-mos through the lens of ecology—*oikos,* meaning "family household," and *logy,* meaning "study of"—is to live in bold opposition to those forces that would have us be disconnected and alone. We cannot, for example, adjust the temperature in our household to suit our comfort without that decision affecting other lives who dwell or visit there. That connection between self and "everything other" is a heavy responsibility and a glorious gift.

Chaos can have a troubling effect on the soul; the saints reveal that a soul can have a soothing effect on chaos. Mindfulness—a quality the saints encourage us to nurture—is vigilance over the soul's condition, and discernment about what in our surroundings disturbs and what stills. But there is more. We are told in Holy Scripture that those who were attracted to Christ came not because of His appearance, but because He had the presence of a god. He is Truth, and people reacted to the Truth: some were drawn, some were repulsed. He is Life, and those who recognized their need for life drank deeply from that Fountain. Jesus, says St. John, is "the light shining in the darkness" (John 1:5).

This influence of soul on surroundings—especially the way a peaceful soul can pacify a raging world—was made real to me by an experience involving one of Valaam's satellite islands. Almost one kilometer from the northwestern edge of Valaam's main island begins the sharp and rocky shoreline of Svyatoi (Holy) Island. The lake around the shore is anything but gentle. Given the position of Svyatoi Island in a constant crosscurrent of turbulent wind, boats can rarely approach the island with safety. Visitors are often left to admire it from a distance.

What is missed, though, is the opportunity to enter one of Valaam's most mysterious and austere places. In the mid-fourteenth century, a skete was founded on the island. A log building with a belfry in one dome remains, as do a hexahedral well and a wooden gallery along the northern shore. A large three-bar cross stands on a shelf of rocks, blessing a thick grove of trees below. Svyatoi Island was once home to eight monks who followed a strict rule. Services were held in the temple on holy days, and on working days, the Psalter was read continuously. Tunneled into the rocks beneath the cross is a cell so small that only one stooping person may enter. He who lived there, we were told, possessed a soul of peace.

When our pilgrimage group was told of the plan for us to visit the island, we were thrilled. When told how threatened such plans are by the island's rough shores, we were saddened. Deacon James said he would approach one man on Valaam's main island "to request permission." Odd, I thought. Even if every one of Valaam's monks bid an enthusiastic farewell, no monk could emerge on deck and command the waves of the sea to be still. Lake Ladoga can be fierce, and if it were so inclined, the best we pilgrims could hope for would be to admire a distant Svyatoi Island through the lens of a camera.

One evening before dusk, Deacon James gathered most of us on the dock. We boarded a boat and sailed north, then west around the main island. Word spread that Deacon James had received a blessing to visit Svyatoi Island. In fact, word spread quietly and with great reverence. As we moved softly on the water, not a single pilgrim spoke above a whisper. Lake Ladoga had not offered a moment's respite from its customary turbulence since our group first arrived at Valaam—until now. With an early evening foggy goldness hovering over the scene, our boat slipped easily through the still waters. We were sailing on flat liquid glass that had not a ripple nor a wave.

Deacon James seemed unsurprised. After all, he had received a blessing to visit Svyatoi Island from Elder Raphael, the monastery's *staretz,* who suddenly became an object of our fascination.

CHAPTER 9

RAPHAEL: ASTONISHMENT

A conversation peppered with the language of the Orthodox Church will not get very far before the word "saint" is uttered. I hold these conversations with some regularity, so use of the word might be about as close to sainthood as I'll ever get. But never to separate oneself from the Church is never to separate oneself from the saints. Who are these people? What qualifies one for sainthood, anyway? Like stars that shine far out of reach, the saints seem to dwell on that horizon that is visible and tangible only in the icons that represent them. And although I don't know the complicated mechanisms behind adding the name of a godly man or woman to the official canon of Orthodox saints, I at least know why the saints are important. I know this because I met a man named Raphael.

He is named after the archangel in the Book of Tobit, one of the Deuterocanonical books of the Old Testament, and his name means "God has healed." His distinction at Valaam is that of an elder, or *staretz* in Russian, and his impact on my life will outlast even my memory of him.

Raphael gave fine and precious detail to the mysterious figure of the elder that emerges from the landscape of Orthodox monasticism and the pages of Russian novels. An elder is one whom the Holy Spirit has nurtured and set apart to possess deep wisdom and discernment and who, by extension, has the gift of guiding others. He is the one to whom many of the other monks go for the Sacrament of Confession, and his finger rests on the spiritual pulse of the monastery. Elders do not campaign for the job; they emerge. From the thousands who confront the temptations of this world, and who enter the monastic life in order to grab their wayward hearts and resolutely offer them back to God, only a rare few reveal the firmest grip and the fiercest resolve. It is from these, then, that an elder emerges by the grace of the Holy Spirit to encourage us all.

It was only after I arrived at Valaam that I learned of Elder Raphael. The stories relayed to us by our trip leader, Deacon James, were of a man about whom little is known, but through whom much is revealed. He is a living example, we were told, of what happens when the Gospel is taken seriously. The most important part of his story, though, is less in where he came from than in who he is. Monks treasure their anonymity. But being a curious American who wants to see the blueprint behind the burning bush, I pressed for what little history was available.

Having come from the tradition of Orthodox monasticism, Elder Raphael is firmly woven into its fabric. For twenty-five years he was a monk at St. Sergius Lavra monastery north of Moscow; for ten years, a hermit in the Caucasus Mountains that edge the border of southwestern Russia between the Black Sea and its eastern neighbor, the Caspian Sea. Seclusion, in Orthodox monasticism, is the condition of the hermit. Too, it is often a prerequisite for gaining the sharp discernment needed to distinguish the truth from the lies of this world, and to shepherd others accordingly. One nineteenth-century figure—

St. Theophan the Recluse—lived in isolation for twenty-seven years, and was rewarded with a deep and full understanding of all that plagues the modern soul and all that is efficacious within the Church to heal it. From this tradition of seclusion, this pure silence and sound that is the choir of nature, Elder Raphael emerges to announce that contemplation is an obligation of every follower of Christ.

Jesus announced that the Kingdom of God is within us, but we are a people emphatically in exile. And contemplation—entering into ourselves in order to attain that Kingdom—is a troubling endeavor, for it is not always easy to tell the difference between *entering* and *indulging*. Humility leads to entering; pride, to indulging and toward a very different kind of kingdom.

At his particular time and place in history, Elder Raphael found contemplation attacked by chaos. The solitary life, it seems, can be a crowded one, for it is populated by the monk and the demons seeking to destroy him. Communism's reputation for hating the Orthodox Church was amplified when Soviet helicopters routinely showered the monastery with machine-gun fire. Accepting the invitation of the abbot of Valaam, Elder Raphael moved north in the spring of 1993 to a more peaceful environment and assumed the role of spiritual director to the monks, and also to the peasants scattered around the island. He settled into a small hut near a chapel known as All Saints, and continued his journey inward.

When our group arrived on the island, our first order of business was to visit Elder Raphael. Initially, our visit was simply a welcome reprieve from the bumpy bus ride that shuttled us from the dock on Lake Ladoga to Valaam's main church. But as we neared the skete, something else took over.

Like the gawking tourists we pretended not to be but

obviously were, each of us pressed his face against the windows on the left side of the old bus to get a glimpse of this holy man. When I first laid eyes on Elder Raphael, he was fleeing. Or, rather, he was moving from the garden for which he cared toward the chapel into which he retreated when nosy people like us came around. Deacon James hastily explained that the elder was no stranger to the intrusion of cameras and flashbulbs. Our driver opened his window as the bus rolled to a stop. Shouting a few indistinguishable words in Russian, he attempted to get Elder Raphael's attention. No luck. The driver then opened his door and jogged toward that small cloaked figure, still negotiating a settlement in Russian. Then, Elder Raphael heard and turned around. The good monk, we discovered, had been expecting us.

Paint a composite portrait of a monk from the minds of men, and we're likely to see a fat oldster with a long bushy beard. He might have a stern expression that is the residue of his ascetic labors, or maybe his shoulders are bent under burdens we don't understand. Elder Raphael was none of this. When he heard from the bus driver that we were the Americans who had come to help restore the monastery, he moved toward us with a step that was light and purposeful. Our group filed from the bus one by one, all of us sensing the presence of the very spirituality we had come to find.

Elder Raphael stood ready to receive us. He was a short man, dressed in a black cassock and wearing the traditional stole, or *schema,* of the elder. A walking stick in his left hand, his right hand was free to grant to each of his pilgrims the blessing of the sign of the cross. Strands of shoulder-length dark hair escaped the cap crowning his head. His face—round and wrinkled and hairless—revealed a sweetness that grew from years of smiles. And then there were his eyes. Wide and wild and lit with love, his eyes seemed privileged with the kind of pure seeing possessed only by the pure in heart. His lone threatening feature was what I imagined he could see in me.

We moved through our days at Valaam in anticipation of seeing Elder Raphael. Only rarely did he emerge from his hut-and-garden home and walk to the main church, usually for a special service. But even his absence had a curious effect on me. More than a few evenings I rested on a log near our campfire feeling reassured—almost protected—because somewhere out there, in or beyond the forest, was Elder Raphael. The light of Christ through him seemed to weaken the darkness, while demons stayed occupied with second thoughts.

This beloved elder became for me the personification of the Gospel. Spiritual speech that is lofty and laden with esoterica so often fails to have an incarnational dimension in our lives. Or, rather, it is we who fail to live by the very words we use in our spiritual conversations. If, as Christ assures us, we will be judged by the words we use, then I definitely need to be on speaking terms with silence. I can encourage or even admonish my brother to set aside what hinders him, but have I set aside what hinders me? Every detail about Elder Raphael delivered the message that he has *earned* the privilege to encourage, to admonish, to speak of spiritual things at all. He loves God and lives his life as if he loves God.

There was, then, a thoroughness to his life. When he came around, other monks would edge by the abbot and jockey for a blessing from the elder's weathered hand. Elder Raphael became a clear and powerful demonstration of *integrity*. His efforts to integrate his love for God with everything he did and said simply gave off an aura of authenticity. It didn't matter that our contact with him was limited; his holiness was not a facade that could be raised and lowered at a moment's notice.

It had been worked and worked into his being through the tools that the Church has given to all of us. Elder Raphael, then, is a Christian not of a different kind, but of a different degree.

And therein lies a key reason for the existence of monasticism. That glorious shock wave that emanates from the Incarnation—God became Man!—established a relationship between heaven and earth, between spirit and matter: "And the Word became flesh and dwelt among us" (John 1:14). We are a people who yearn to taste and see, who are invited by God Himself not just to imagine Him, but to experience Him. Within the walls of a monastery are men or women who strive to realize fully—to incarnate—the Gospel of Christ in their lives. They are sinners like us, seeking freedom. And when they venture from the monastery in their monastic garb, we can look upon them and know that they are striving to set aside all earthly cares to attain salvation. Elder Raphael, as a human being, reveals to this human being that the Gospel of Christ is not a remote world of words and ideas, but is real and reachable and transforming.

Ours is a horizontal age—flat with no real depth. Physical, emotional, and spiritual maturity are painfully scarce. Without the guidance of mentors, young boys are left to initiate themselves into manhood, and young girls twist at the mercy of an exploiting culture. The rites of initiation have played a crucial role in traditional cultures because those cultures have, in definable ways, loved their young. America may worship youthfulness, but it does not really love its young. Indeed, in our culture the killing of an unborn child is considered reasonable payment to preserve a "youthful" lifestyle of freedom, individuality, and pursuit of happiness. We sacrifice our young to stay young.

But when I experienced the culture of Valaam Monastery, "young" and "old" assumed clearer and more powerful meanings than I had known. Elder Raphael was not an elder because he was old in age, but because he was holy. It so happens, though, that holiness takes experience, and experience takes time. When a person enters monastic life, there is a deliberate leaving of his former self, of the former ways of living, and of the virtues and sins of his past. A new relationship is formed with God, and also with himself. He is born into a progressive existence in which his growth is not determined exclusively by his own understanding, but by the wisdom and discernment of his *abbot,* a word that means "father." It was encouraging to learn that Elder Raphael had made the spiritual journey from birth to maturity—that one pilgrimage to which we are all called.

One enters the monastic life as a *novice.* He is given only a portion of the monastic habit—usually a tunic, a leather belt, and a headdress known as a *skoufos* for men, or *apostolnik* for women, to wear as an expression of his decision to live as a monk. After a period of time in which the novice matures in the Christian life to the satisfaction of the abbot, he may receive an additional garment worn by a *ryasophore,* one who is in the next stage of monastic life. The novice becomes a ryasophore by an appropriate rite in church performed by a priest-monk—the very rite our group witnessed when the two novices crawled the length of the nave floor to the altar. This progression has an important public dimension for the new monk because his conscience combines with the witness of the community to impose upon him his obligation to continue in the monastic life for the rest of his days.

So the monk is growing. By his speech, his silence, his behavior, his confessions, his repentance, he is revealing to his spiritual father that he is bringing more and more of his life under the lordship of Christ. He may progress to the rank of *stavrophore,* a Greek word meaning "cross-bearer." The monk now receives a wooden cross to be worn at all times, and a long flowing cloak to be worn only in church.

This progression, too, is accompanied by an imposing and sober rite in which the monk is given a new name, signifying the death of the old man and the putting on of the new. This new name is accepted, not chosen. And this act of obedience may lead in time to fuller obedience to God in thought, word, and deed, and to the rank of *megaloschemos.* Now, a greater degree of asceticism is required. The distinctive color of his raiment is black, symbolizing repentance. The monk realizes that his life of repentance will end only when he exhales his last breath.

A remarkable characteristic of this monastic progression is that it is not guaranteed. There is no certainty nor necessity that one will advance from one stage to another. And in the colorful history of Orthodox monasticism, there have been some novices who shone with the wisdom of an elder, and some elders who simply should have remained novices. But this ancient system of accountability has a kind of intrinsic sanity, for it is based on fundamental truths about the human personality: we are not as strong as we think we are; the soul is too precious to leave untended; too much freedom can be harmful; we discover our uniqueness while in relationship with others; and timing is critical. A monk sees himself in the mirror of others while an elder with purer vision explains to him what is being seen, and how to cleanse the image. To grow in the spiritual life, then, is to see more clearly the image of God in others and in oneself.

We pilgrims came to Valaam Monastery and were disillusioned. What a blessing! Any illusions of "believing in yourself" fell from our eyes—even if temporarily—and we caught a glimpse of our true condition as sinners and our true position as the beloved of God. There is a time and a season, I learned, to all things. My thirst to be an expert at something by the age of twenty-five would certainly go unsatisfied. And it should. I have rarely lived life with the patience, the practicality, the simple and consistent labor that is less art, and more *craft*. St. Paul encouraged each pilgrim in the church at Thessalonica toward this kind of maturity when he wrote that they should "aspire to lead a quiet life, to mind your own business, and to work with your own hands" (1 Thessalonians 4:11). For my part, Elder Raphael helped me toward this sacred condition by granting me, among others, the opportunity to have a private conversation with him.

I had been living my days at Valaam in a swirl of ideas and experiences. The stimulus was there; the response was forthcoming. We were nearing the end of our pilgrimage, and it remained unclear how much of Valaam I would take back to America. Deacon James confirmed what we had heard unofficially: Elder Raphael would visit our small island to witness our renovation work and to speak with us individually. Orthodox Christians believe that when an elder speaks, he uses the language of God. Choose your questions carefully, Deacon James admonished, for you may not like what you hear.

Several of us followed Deacon James and Elder Raphael on the path from the large cross on the cliff to the small chapel. We walked in silence. I inventoried my experiences and tried to choose several that needed light and clarity. Each of us slipped through the maze of boards and scaffolding that cloaked the old chapel and gingerly made his way across the muddied planks that provided the only entry. Deacon James told us pilgrims to wait outside and take turns speaking with Elder Raphael.

One at a time, we were told, one at a time. I entered the church and noticed an uneven triangle formed between Elder Raphael, Deacon James, and an empty chair. Both the elder and the deacon were seated on the floor. Sunlight spilled through the spaces in the walls and covered the floor in long bright lines and small golden circles. Nervously, I sat down.

One may get a vague feeling of nervousness when he realizes that his secrets are about to become conversations. But when the uncovering happens in a context of love and mercy, a healthy shame emerges. We take responsibility for what we have done with the image of God in our lives, and we wonderfully discover that our misdeeds do not have to destroy us. Instead, the True Light shines, and our shadows starve, then disappear.

I was the first to speak. Offering my case in short choppy sentences for Deacon James to translate from English to Russian, I mostly stared at the floor. Those dusty boards were a less threatening audience than the wide penetrating eyes of the elder. Our time together absorbed only twenty minutes—the power of that time lay not in its length, but in its depth. And I noticed, afterward, that my conversation had contained more about my future than my past. It was not so much a confession as it was a hunger for guidance.

Elder Raphael listened patiently. He occasionally nodded in affirmation as he received the translation from Deacon James. Finally, Elder Raphael responded in his high-pitched and quiet voice with words that seeped like sweet water into the cracks and details of my questions. He spoke of thankfulness to God. He spoke of never failing to give God all the glory given to me. And he challenged me to live in the threefold discipline of chastity, humility, and prayer. It was a discipline, I would soon discover, crucial for my survival when I arrived back in my home country.

The light and dust hung suspended around the three of us in that chapel. Those and other elements—shade, color, contrast, clothing, the coolness in the air—combined to form a supporting role. Everything seemed near and alive, but wholly powerless to distract from a single syllable of the elder's words. As those words were translated into English, I wrote them down.

After all, they contained pure Gospel from a man who has taken it seriously.

Later that evening as the campfire danced, a friend who had also had a conversation with Elder Raphael described its wake: "It is like an axis has been driven into your life, and you are left to determine how your life will revolve around it." Yes, he is correct. An encounter with Elder Raphael may reveal a clear and brilliantly lit path, the very one you have been patiently seeking. Or, it may not. The gift one gets may simply be permission to go on struggling. We seek guidance, and sometimes receive it; we seek relief, and sometimes receive only the encouragement to keep fighting the good fight.

Through the fire's embers that split the darkness like spiraling stars, my eyes surveyed the black outline of the nearby forest. Occasionally it feels as though the world has an overwhelming power to crush us; that is, if our human nature doesn't finish us off first. But there is absolutely no sound promise offered from the circles of holiness that life is free from struggle. To struggle is to engage, and to engage the spiritual life is one of the few worthy pursuits of man. I stare into the night and wonder if the persistent darkness in my life is evidence not of my struggling, but of the absence of struggling.

"Woe to you *who are* at ease in Zion" (Amos 6:1)—quite unlike the remarkable man who is out there, somewhere, moving among the deep woods.

CHAPTER 10

JOHN THE BAPTIST: SUDDENNESS

Scan the pages of the New Testament in search of a patron saint of monasticism, and one figure rises from his meal of locusts and honey to assume the role—John the Baptist. There is something special about this man. Even before his parents, Zechariah and Elizabeth, joined in the blessed union that began his life, St. John's name was a record in heaven revealed to earth. And the same angel of the Annunciation delivered to St. John's father more than just the boy's name: St. John, we are told by the Apostle Luke, "will be filled with the Holy Spirit, even from his mother's womb" (Luke 1:15).

The Tradition of the Christian Church elaborates on the significance of St. John's birth. We discover that his parents aren't the only ones who notice his arrival. "Desert, rejoice!" and "All creation, the entire earth, is filled with joy!" shout the liturgical hymns associated with his entrance upon the world stage. The portrait of St. John that emerges from the Gospels is that of a sane man who lives as if he is mad. His toned and disciplined body is dirtied with the matter of earth—sand, animal hair, vegetation. He dwells not in the dizzying centers of commerce, but in the desolate spaces of caves and open desert. We do not quite see him as a loner, but as a man who will only move in company as fiercely single-minded as he. He is not diplomatic, but deeply humane.

St. John takes each step through the Gospel narrative with the strength of generations of Hebrew prophets behind him. Specifically, we are told that he comes in "the spirit and power of Elijah" (Luke 1:17). That prophet was a burning flame who engulfed idolatrous Israel and its wicked king in a spoken truth that was unrelenting, unambiguous, and untamed. So we are not surprised when John the Baptist delivers a similar blow to the gut of the Jordanian community. He is not polite, but he is loving enough to passionately call for people to do what is best for themselves: "Bear fruits worthy of repentance" (Luke 3:8). His advice is timeless.

The biblical texts devoted to St. John reveal not only a deep vocation to his life, but his keen awareness of it. He voluntarily dwells in the desert—a landscape of shadowy death that compels a man to cling to the necessities of life. And what emerges from the pages of those texts is that what is necessary for life is more than food and drink. St. John is more interested in the soul than in the stomach. Our Lord tells us that the Baptist "came neither eating bread nor drinking wine" (Luke 7:33). There is, to St. John's life, a conspicuous absence of frivolity and of wasted time. He is not a "reed shaken by the wind" who conforms to the whims and trends of his culture, nor is he one "clothed in soft garments" who cavorts among the prestigious and powerful (Luke 7:24, 25). No, St. John lives simply and close to the earth. He is acquainted with the basic wisdom of nature. And he recognizes that Wisdom even from a distance when He comes to him to be baptized.

John the Baptist reveals his monastic character in the desert where he dwells, in the fierce single-mindedness of his vocation, but also in his role as a Forerunner to the Messiah. A troparion—a short, poetic hymn extolling the virtue of a saint or a saving event—was composed centuries ago for St. John and shares the significance of his coming:

> The memory of the just is celebrated with hymns of
>   praise,
> But the Lord's testimony is enough for thee,
>   O Forerunner,
> For thou wast granted to baptize in the running
>   waters
> Him whom thou didst proclaim.
> Then having endured great suffering for the Truth,
> Thou didst rejoice to bring, even to those in Hell,
> The good tidings that God had appeared in the flesh,
> To take away the sins of the world,
> And to grant to us all His great mercy.

St. John's voice echoed off the orange walls of desert rock, through dry brushweed and over hot sand. In wide spaces of sparse fertility, his message found its way into the moist and ready hearts of those hungry for a new Kingdom. As messengers go, John the Baptist sure could draw a crowd. St. Mark tells us that "all the land of Judea, and those from Jerusalem, went out to him and were all baptized by him in the Jordan River, confessing their sins" (Mark 1:5). People drawn to St. John must have been the kind who were ready to trust a promise. "I am not the One for whom you seek," he announces with conviction, "but after me comes One more powerful than I, the thongs of whose sandals I am not worthy to stoop down and untie." He tells his followers to wait a little longer, not in idleness but in a spirit of preparation. Jesus is coming.

St. John's message now falls from the lips and lifestyles of the Christian monastic community. Monks and nuns gather in wilderness—revealed both in the physical world of nature and the spiritual wasteland of cities—to shed distractions; they shed distractions to focus on a single goal; they focus on a single goal to save themselves and others. The monastery, the mission, the message—all these amount to an announcement: Jesus is coming. And "His winnowing fork *is* in His hand, and He will thoroughly clean out His threshing floor, and gather His wheat into the barn, but He will burn up the chaff with unquenchable fire" (Matthew 3:12). All monastic activity—prayer, work, good deeds, participation in the sacraments—is intended to draw attention not to him who does them, but to Him who receives them. The monk becomes a forerunner of Jesus.

The association of monastic life with St. John the Baptist is one I did not make until the end of my pilgrimage to Valaam Monastery. His name never came up. Our group became familiar with the saints who have a direct connection with Valaam—Sergius and Herman, Herman of Alaska, even Seraphim of Sarov. But I didn't encounter St. John, at least in conversation, until the day before we left the monastery. Now, I consider him as close as a brother. We were formally introduced by an Orthodox nun in an abrupt meeting on a thin trail through the forest leading to an outhouse.

Our group's focus was shifting from renovation work to preparing to leave the monastery. It was a warm Monday, warm but not hot. The temperature and weather conditions were perfectly suited to turn my walk in the woods into a stroll. But it was a stroll with purpose; breakfast had been served several hours earlier and the outhouse was about a hundred yards away.

I drifted from the open camp into the shade of the forest canopy's first branches. The main trail, like most, was wide-mouthed, then narrowed as tree trunks closed in and lined both sides. It was always a nice moment—moving from direct sunlight into cool shade. Movement was light and easy for this frame that had shed more than a few pounds by hauling logs up this very trail. Twenty yards from the open camp, the trail had a southern sidetrack that wandered through dense trees and eventually spilled onto a rocky shore. Halfway between the start of the sidetrack and the shore was the only outhouse on the island. It had two separate facilities, in case of heavy traffic.

I turned south and looked up. A wash of green hung suspended on tall brown trunks and allowed only slivers of sunlight to dot the forest floor. This, I thought, is what I've come to love about monastery life. Yes, such richness is available elsewhere, but I couldn't remember ever *gazing* at creation. Valaam reminded me not to ignore the immediate world around me as if it were incidental, but to look at these trees, this trail, that water, these people, with a heart open to what makes them beautiful.

My gaze shifted and settled on a lone figure walking in my direction. It was Sister Maria. She was returning either from the outhouse or the shore, for those were the only two options on this trail. An active woman on this trip, she had participated in many tasks ranging from pouring concrete to pouring pancake batter. I recognized her potato-shape moving well through the trees. As she neared, I searched my memory for what I knew of her, but the data were slim. I knew she had been an Orthodox nun at one time, but I couldn't remember if she was still active in that role or if she had shifted her ascetic effort to care for a family. Finally, we drew near enough to each other not to have to raise our voices to be heard.

"Perfect day, isn't it?" I asked.

"Indeed! I can't believe it hasn't rained at all since we've been here." Sister Maria targeted a well-worn item of conversation on our pilgrimage—the lack of rain during northern Russia's rainy season. She had a pleasant conversational quality about her, quick with wit and a good story. Her phrases did not come gently, but with a slightly anxious quality. She didn't act agitated, just . . . preoccupied. Here was a woman, I thought, who has accomplished much and who believes she has much left to accomplish.

It happened suddenly. "Where are you going after you leave here?" she asked, eyes drilled straight into mine.

"Uh, I'm going back to America, to Tennessee."

"Is there a church there?"

"Yes," I replied.

"Will you go?"

"Yes."

"Every Sunday?"

I had the clear feeling that Sister Maria was entering into a monologue. It was her job to talk, mine to listen. She had known that I was a musician, and that I had planned to go to Tennessee to nurture my interest in that profession. It was a career decision that must be made with sharpest discernment, Sister Maria surmised, because it can be particularly damaging to the soul. She had known a few artists in her time and was aware of the hazy line between art as an expression of the soul and art as an extension of the ego. Too, she knew that people often admire artists for the wrong reasons.

"You're attractive, and that's not a blessing." Sister Maria continued to surprise me. She explained that anything that draws attention away from the state of the soul and toward the appetite of the flesh is dangerous. "Music is a wonderful thing, but your profession, that industry, is a difficult place to be a Christian. People don't know that adoration for anything or anyone other than God is harmful."

That adoration is always to be a vertical expression—man to God—was something I understood. But Sister Maria was speaking to me in what felt like an island within an island. As she spoke, the world suddenly grew small, and I forgot about the forest and the sun and began staring at her mouth. I listened to her words and felt the conviction behind them. She did not speak loudly or even forcibly, just clearly. I understood that I was not to speak even in the pauses between her sentences.

I knew she was right. Music is an art often more powerful than a strictly visual medium, especially when more than one sense is involved. To see a portrait can be moving; to hear and see music performed can be gripping. The creative process is visible and audible. "Next to the Word of God," wrote Martin Luther, "music deserves the highest praise." Sister Maria was cautioning me to enter into that creative process with a strong sense of right and wrong, of humility and even humor. It has killed many a man's soul, she said.

"Who's your patron saint?" she asked suddenly and after a long pause. I panicked in thought. I didn't have one! Somehow the selection of a patron saint at my baptism got swamped by a thousand other details. But how could I possibly respond to this kind, loving woman that I didn't have one? I stared at her frantically trying to find a reply. Surely my horror was visible.

"Who's your patron saint?" she asked again, "John the Theologian or John the Baptist?" In a sweeping stroke of utter mercy, my choices were narrowed to two. I knew that John the Theologian kept good company with Matthew, Mark, and Luke. In no more than a few seconds, I flashed through everything I knew of John the Theologian. He was superbly qualified. But, for a reason not at all clear to me then or now, he was not my choice.

"St. John the Baptist," I replied with quiet confidence.

"Good," said Sister Maria sweetly, "he didn't take shit from nobody."

I'm not sure what happened next. Perhaps my jaw hit the ground. Leaves and branches probably fell from trees, and animals surely turned their stunned gaze toward Sister Maria as she softly closed her eyes and smiled. She added a few sentences that I think had something to do with the need of being strong. I honestly don't remember.

Some monastics have an earthy quality that makes a sudden appearance. Those appearances are perfect antidotes to the misperception that to be a monk is to be shy, demure, or without humor. Both Sister Maria and her recommendation, John the Baptist, had an edge to their personalities that make dull people like me sit up and take notice. And when that edge appears unexpectedly—a chance meeting in a lovely wood or a long walk through the sparse desert—it cuts through convention and grazes the heart.

I entered the forest alone, but emerged with a companion. St. John the Baptist is a man worthy of emulation: a forerunner of Jesus, a man of prayer, a simple man, a humble spirit, a wilderness-dweller, a baptizer, a crying voice, a prophet who spoke the truth, a martyr, and a monk. He was also a bridge of respect between the two great callings of celibacy and marriage. An ascetic, he died for preaching right relationships. "It is not lawful for you, [Herod,] to have your brother's wife" (Mark 6:18). The patron saint of monasticism was martyred for defending the sanctity of marriage. St. John reveals that these two callings are twin roads leading to the same destination—pure love for God.

St. John even used the language of marriage to draw the figure of Christ into sharp relief:

> You yourselves bear me witness, that I said, 'I am not the Christ,' but, 'I have been sent before Him.' He who has the bride is the bridegroom; but the friend of the bridegroom, who stands and hears him, rejoices greatly because of the bridegroom's voice. Therefore this joy of mine is fulfilled. He must increase, but I *must* decrease. (John 3:28–30)

From the suffocation of his prison cell, St. John remained humble. He seemed to deflect all pity and instead directed his disciples to seek Jesus and ask of Him, "Are you the one?" Finally, John the Baptist was beheaded. The Orthodox Church celebrates the life and death of this man several times throughout the liturgical year—his conception, his baptism of Jesus, his death, even the finding of his head two and three times in the centuries following his martyrdom. His head has been preserved incorrupt.

Donatello, the fifteenth-century Florentine artist, sculpted from marble a John the Baptist whose face was fierce and somber. Yes, I could imagine it. I could imagine a hard life in the desert doing that to a man. But if Donatello could sculpt an image of the heart of this great saint, it would have to be carved from fire.

CHAPTER 11

FAREWELL

Thursday morning, which brought with it our last day at the monastery, arrived as quietly and naturally as had every morning. So little wind, but great sunshine showered our camp and allowed us to feel unencumbered all the emotions that arose with the closing of our pilgrimage. Had there been rain, we could have played in that messy distraction; had it been cold, we could have rationalized amongst ourselves how nice it was to be leaving this chilly place; had it been foggy, we could have pretended that gathering our tools and packing our tents was harder than it really was. But we had been granted the same beautiful sunrise as yesterday, and the day before yesterday. Yes, it was a perfect morning to walk around weeping inside.

So we made noise. My ears awoke before my eyes did. Several yards from my tent, my fellow pilgrims were hastily building a pile of construction supplies to give to the monastery—tool belts, hammers, pliers, a few boxes of nails, semi-new work gloves, even a filthy pair of boots no self-respecting monk would ever wear. These, along with our sins, were the detritus of our journey: leave them here, for it is a long way back to America and they have already served their purpose.

But for all its sweet sameness, this morning stood out from

the others and made every moment and movement just plain difficult. My breakfast was a bitter mixture of dread and longing: I didn't want to leave Valaam, but I missed my family and was eager to return home even though I had no assurance that home was worth returning to. Closing my eyes, I could imagine with painful clarity the coming conflict—settling back into a Western culture hostile toward the truths I had learned on this island, and intolerant of any attempt to live them out.

In the patch of grass where several of us drowsy and disheveled night owls lingered, small talk trickled. The few priests on our trip roused the last of the sleepers and herded our group toward the tall cross for morning prayers. As we walked, no one said much of anything. We had laid a familiar path from our campsite to the cliff and ambled along easily, without the newness that had filled our first few days here. And as before, the springlike scent of spruce trees smelled better to me than brewing coffee. We walked peacefully, but many of us were hurting deeply.

Carelessly we stood around the cross, each trying to soothe and understand his own internal battle of time and distance and devotion: Who am I now? Am I returning home with only dirty laundry and a few stories to show for my pilgrimage? Who was this mysterious monk I met and what should I do with his words? In keeping with my nature, I tried to smooth the edges of this emotional moment by forcing some intellectual separation—*Yes, of course, this is what we do, we are born and we grow up and live our lives and get married and have kids and grow old and every now and then we have experiences like this one at Valaam Monastery and take pieces of those experiences with us and live some more and maybe end our lives in a slight hint of the ideal God had for us when we began.* But it didn't work; some of the best experiences of our lives are those that kindly overwhelm our ability to shut them out.

Our last day. We stood on the cliff and prepared to say our morning prayers. The thousand small eruptions of thought and feeling converged with the steady swirl of wind blowing through the tall grass and tree branches. Lost in that strange sensation of feeling fully present but fully universal, I added my voice to the choir of those praying the ancient prayers that offer thanks to God for a new day. But I couldn't concentrate. And as I would later record in a journal, I couldn't get a grip "on my relationship at this moment with that cross, with this monastery, with these people, and with that culture back home." My imagination moved over space and time to survey the days and months and years ahead, when this pilgrimage would grow ever more remote and cloudy.

And with it, I imagined, would quietly disappear the strength and courage to be steadfast in prayer and fasting like these monks; to love the wilderness and fight the good fight like St. John the Baptist; never again to yield any ground to the slothful side of me; to serve as I have been served; to pray daily for those in my life; and simply to love the way Elder Raphael loves. I could feel the fading coming. We prayed our morning prayers and already I was tasting the dust of defeat. I was far away from where I simply needed to be—at this place, at this time, and in this way.

The words rolled over and among us. One of the most familiar prayers was at hand, and its first few words summoned me back to the ground beneath my feet and to the cross before my eyes. Today, this prayer would weave its pure message through the minutes and moments that tracked my farewell. And like the young man who not too long ago began to feel at home in a temple of the ancient and alive Orthodox Church, I finally and unreservedly entered into the morning prayer:

Grant me, O Lord, to greet this coming day in peace.
Just look at this place. I measure each step and every sight
according to its finality: "This is the last time I'll walk to the
well," or, "This is the last time I'll see this old chapel." Yes, I
am sad, even afraid. But notice, there is absolutely no hint of
melodrama, just hundreds of tiny, natural deaths of sense and
experience that help me understand that this is our last day.
Tomorrow, surely, will have a fullness of its own.

Still, I pray for a peace from above that has so often seemed
elusive. To chase this peace is like chasing this wind that blows
in from the lake, around my body, then back out again. But
the prayer says that peace is not caught, it is accepted. It is
granted to him who is ready to receive, or, by grace, to him
who is at least willing. The coming hours of this day are vague
and haunting; I dread them.

*Help me in all things to rely upon Thy holy will. In every hour of
the day, reveal Thy will to me.*
Our tents bundled, our bags packed, we take turns carrying
gear down to the dock and loading the ferryboat. None of us
having a clue whether to celebrate or cry, we good-naturedly
sing songs and keep conversation light. One remarkable thing
I notice is the swiftness with which I cover this quarter-mile
uphill grade from the dock to the clearing. Surely with the
manual labor, I've lost a few pounds and gained some muscle.
But these monks who've come to our island, they live a life
more strenuous, more constant, than the one we've lived for
these weeks, and still, they're quite fat. Padded cassocks, I imagine—enough insulation to keep out the Cold War.

The big things—job, whom to marry, where to live—yes,
I understand the importance of God's will as the primary vari-
able in making these decisions. But *all* things? Sticks and twigs

and tiny leaves pepper the path and some of the dock. I remember being told that Elder Raphael had a "heart of silence" that was always listening to God, always begging Him for Christlikeness. The Elder, then, could hold a day's worth of conversations and might never say anything that was contrary to the will of God. Words, rest, small tasks and acts—is God that intimate with His creatures?

Bless my dealings with all who surround me.
Every moment, a redemption. Valaam Monastery offers to this pilgrim a glimpse into a Kingdom that is in this world, but not of this world. I am impressed with how the people here spend their time—as if time were a gift; and I am convicted of how I spend mine—as if time were a possession I owned, to do with what I please. So much of my learning has come simply from observing these faithful. They are not time-wasters, but instead stand vigilant for opportunities to do right and to live well. Their behavior contributes something good and redeeming to the day. "Redeem the time," writes St. Paul, "because the days are evil" (Ephesians 5:16).

I notice how much interaction the monks have with each other. Even when they are not in conversation, they are still in community. Each somehow comes across the work, the mess, the possessions, or the evidence left by another. And the teachings of this monastery encourage the monk to take that seriously: be considerate, be kind, do not be petty. Uncomfortably, I address a few instances when I wasn't considerate or kind, but petty, with the pilgrims with whom I have journeyed. The real lesson for me, then, is not necessarily to force acts of kindness on those with whom I come into contact— even that can be a subtle form of self-centeredness—but to be open to what is right and appropriate and timely for our time together. Love is always due, of course, but I must be aware of when it is better not to speak a kind word, but to receive one; not to teach, but to learn; not to initiate, but to honor a more humble path of simply not being noticed.

Teach me to treat all that comes to me throughout the day with peace of soul and with firm conviction that Thy will governs all. I step from the island to the dock and from the dock to the boat. This and other demarcations I will remember as well as I will remember the lines around Elder Raphael's eyes. Many of us, but not all, are sailing away from the island carrying much less baggage than when we arrived. Or, rather, we have exchanged the heavy yoke of our old references, our old slogans, for a lighter but no less intimidating yoke of a fresh new framework. We have received a new way of looking at ourselves, our families, and the circumstances waiting to meet us just two days from now. But just as when receiving the fullness of the Faith itself, this richer worldview comes with the exacting price of obedience. I feel the wind on my face as we pull away from the dock; fresh air will not purify unless one breathes deeply.

Out upon the bumpy waters of Lake Ladoga. Such a sweet dynamic it is to face this beautiful monastery fading from view, only to turn around to face the spotless horizon with its miles and miles of water and sky. Thanks be to God, I have won completely: Behind me lay an experience nuanced with hundreds of life-changing possibilities; ahead of me lies a life of possibility waiting to be experienced. But I cannot deny that even this poignant moment is not without stain. We move upon the waters and so much is rootless, still. Questions of identity and role surface when I consider going home. Peace of soul, though, peace of soul.

In all my deeds and words, guide my thoughts and feelings.
Deacon James wanders to where I am standing near the bow of the boat and mentions that our renovation of Valaam has made news all over Russia. The prime minister of the country would soon visit to see for himself. Though charmed that I'd come so close to international headlines, I chuckle that a quiet work among quiet people could make such noise. It is clear now that many of us pilgrims had no idea why we came to Valaam. I could walk the length of this boat, interrogate the passengers, and from each probably learn a unique motivation. Many of us leapt first, and then the net appeared.

The drone of the boat's engine isn't as noticeable now. I stand steadily and absorb the expressions on the faces. Love, I have been told, is more *doing* than anything else. Not the weak pandering to every mood—"I must do what I feel"—no, that invites self-destruction; but love as an act of the will toward what is right and true. Love is a willful act even when the internal mood has turned dark and unloving, or simply ambiguous. The towering saints of the Church were common men and women whose wills were in advanced stages of healing.

My friend Ben, leaning there against the rope railings, is learning to love. This young and curious boy had other, more entertaining, offers of how to spend his summer vacation. But even in his confusion of options and inclinations, he chose the way of love. The Valaam pilgrimage was good for him, he assumed, so he denied himself the pleasure of a few weeks at a California beach and accepted a time of dirt, sweat, bad food, and long church services. Ben chose not what his body wanted but what his soul craved—hard work and mystery. Good for you, Ben, for loving your soul.

So we choose the way of love, yet often communicate to

the world how unhappy we are with our choice. I know about complaining, for I have done my share. It has been said that all successful transactions with the psyche involve deals, as if we say to ourselves, "If you let me work hard for one hour, I'll let you be lazy for one hour." Our acts of love sometimes carry the unloving condition of subtle payback. I have more than once on this trip sacrificed for a fellow pilgrim only to either avoid him later so I wouldn't have to sacrifice again, or let my discomfort with sacrifice escape in the form of unloving thoughts. When will I learn that my thoughts and feelings are just as precious and important to God as my deeds and words? That they are another frontier to conquer, another piece to yield?

In unforeseen events, let me not forget that all are sent by Thee.
It has been several hours since we set sail. The waters of Lake Ladoga are especially choppy as we near our rendezvous on land with two buses that will carry us back to St. Petersburg tonight. The dry, stable land feels good, and this outpost is an attractive, though desolate, place. Abruptly, Deacon James closes a conversation with a Russian man and is visibly upset. The unspoken hierarchy of communication in our group hums as Deacon James relays information privately to the few priests, who then inform us that our transportation won't arrive until tomorrow. Okay, now what? Even after exposure to the blessed simplicity of Valaam, I want a hotel. But this outpost offers only a few cabins and a tiny, one-room locked chapel. Here, in a group of twenty, I am starting to feel alone.

Two hours pass. The sun bids farewell and drifts below the horizon, taking the warmth with it. As most groups do when hungry and a little fearful, we let slip occasional eruptions of anger. I see a few troubled faces, hear a few raised voices and heavy sighs. Some of the younger men cope by finding a chunk of rubber and building a football game around it. Most of us, though, either keep to ourselves or stand in company wishing we had. Judging by my own irritability toward this rough transition, I must have had clear and rigid expectations. So once again, that god had to fall.

The elder spoke of being thankful in every context; St. Paul wrote of being content in every situation. In conversations with a few of the monks, they would often utter "thanks be to God" after sharing the details of an unpleasant experience. These lessons come to me tonight as I sit on this log by a fire. Cold, hungry, tired, irritable . . . and thankful? Word comes that we've opened the cabins and found beds and covers. Before we settle in for the night, Deacon James has found the key to the lock that hangs on the chapel door. Dozens of candles are lit, and as I enter I smell incense seeping faintly from the wood walls. Yes, this place was built for one purpose. Only eight or ten of us can fit into the chapel at one time, so we take turns praying and singing. Our spirits change, soften. And the conditions become right for an important work— reflection. I will remember where I have been and consider where I am going. Had I been in a noisy bus with chatty cargo, headed toward somewhere comfortable, I'm not convinced that I would have cared.

Teach me to act firmly and wisely, without embittering and embarrassing others.
As we settle down for the evening, I survey a landscape losing its detail to the setting sun.

I have seen a sunset like this before—on the southern edge of the island. It was there, on rocks that had been smoothed by the steady cycle of tides, where I closed my eyes and concentrated on drawing the deepest breath I could hold. Yes, hold it . . . hold it . . . let Valaam do its interior work. My only regret was having to exhale.

A human wears the marks of his soul on the outside. In fact, he can't help it. Like a tree whose roots take nourishment from good soil or bad, he will be known by the fruit he bears. A neglected soul, one that has not been pruned by ascetic effort, will have no definition. And such a person will often wander through life timid and detached from the richness of life's varied experiences. A great tragedy, then, is that he will see the world as shallow and formless, never considering that it isn't the world he sees, but his own soul.

Discovering an identity for the soul requires the hard work of discipline and the sustained work of prayer. It requires initiative. And it requires resolve, such as the kind that may cause a few hurt feelings in those who may—intentionally or not—have an interest in keeping your soul formless. But this holy fierceness is grounded as much in discernment as in determination. To mitigate the spirit of fear that numbs the soul too easily and too often, God grants to His people "a spirit of power and of love and of a sound mind," as St. Paul explains in 2 Timothy 1:7. Power without love or a sound mind leads to savagery; the earth and its people have too many bruises as proof.

C. S. Lewis observed that one human being is infinitely more important than the whole universe because the human will live forever. It follows, then, that our real saving work on earth involves relationships. To exercise proper spiritual fortitude is not to run roughshod over a friend, a stranger, a colleague, a spouse, a relative, a poor man, or a fool. Rather, it is to fight *for* them, for the health and dignity of my relationship with them. I remember a small sign my mother gave me years ago. The words, written by Philo of Alexandria, are simple but powerful: "Be kind; everyone you meet is fighting a hard battle."

Give me strength to bear the fatigue of the coming day, with all that it shall bring.
The bunk is not uncomfortable, and my sleeping bag is sufficient cushion. The noise from my roommates softens, then fades as we quickly discover how tired we all are. I pass time by imagining what will happen to a few of these new friends when they return home and resume their lives.

To each, though, I wish strength. That the life of faith is an everyday walk is understood by anyone who has tried to live it. Circumstances happen that aren't favorable, distractions reach over and tug at our chins, and when we aren't besieged by forces outside us, we are betrayed by forces within. Strength for the journey is what we are promised by Christ Himself—"Lo, I am with you always, *even* to the end of the age" (Matthew 28:20). It is He who completes the everyday walk of faith in us; the strength is in His legs, not ours. And the Savior instructs us that to worry about tomorrow is simply a waste of time. We cannot change the fine details of a single moment, save the one we are in.

Direct my will, teach me to pray. And Thyself, pray in me. Amen.
To a peaceful close, the day fades. And look, I am the same flawed human who started this morning, and will start tomorrow. But I am also the same hopeful man who calls to God for help. Once again, the Holy Scriptures offer insight into how God helps and from where comes even the inclination to stretch forth my hand to receive it. "For it is God who works in you," St. Paul reminds the Philippians and this

pilgrim, "both to will and to do for *His* good pleasure" (Philippians 2:13).

Yes, it is You who wish to direct my will, and yet are willing to be sorrowed by it; in whom I live and move and have my being, however pained by that very intimacy. Your grace is poured upon this cold miser who rarely offers even the slightest word of thanks. Still, on that cross rests the blood of God. Tonight, even if my tired mind sprang sharp and wild, never could I grasp the endless sky of Your love.

So the dark falls and I hear the soft drone of sleepers breathing. By this time tomorrow I will have traveled a few thousand miles and taken my first sip of American air in weeks. During a yawn I make the sign of the cross over myself, making certain to touch my formed hand to the sleeping bag over my stomach and shoulders. Tomorrow will be a long day, and it is one journey I cannot make alone.

We had come to Valaam to see, and to learn how to see. The world—I have been told by those whose spiritual paths are as deep and rich as ocean life—is alive and full of glory. The world, too, is full of danger and ugliness and temptation. Those monks settled at Valaam not to flee from the world, but to flee from worldliness. And to confront their portions of all the glory and deception and greatness and evil that lie in the hearts of every human being. He is the brave one who steps from the noisy, blurry distractions of worldly life just long enough to discover that his most desperate need is, in fact, unmeetable by any measure of his own. Though plentiful gods abound, eager to step in, they are hollow. Only Jesus Christ can make a person new and whole and sane.

CHAPTER 12

FROM ETERNITY TO HERE

Were I to be leaving Valaam six months later, my journey would begin during a day of almost perpetual darkness. Valaam in winter is a rugged place. Only the clarity of the night sky competes with the freezing temperatures for attention. With no haze of electric lights in the air above, stars of all sizes hang twinkling like millions of fresh drops of silver paint sprayed on a wide black canvas.

Our group leaves the island and travels to St. Petersburg. There, each pilgrim follows his path that will lead back to America. I linger in the city long enough to taste its culture before leaving for Finland. Right now, it is easy to feel as if the universe contains only two places—Valaam and everywhere else. All that is not Valaam seems tightly bound together in a blur of traffic, smog, bustle, noise, buildings, clocks, technology, information, concrete, televisions, and food. I feel like fleeing.

The transition from the stillness of Valaam to the circus of Babylon shakes me hard. The sheer volume of activity—some of it profane, most of it busy, all of it distracting—that I encounter after leaving the island feels abrasive, like rubbing the back of a smooth hand against sharp facial stubble. Along the streets of St. Petersburg, the shouting vendors and many magazines offer no shortage of other things on which to dwell than the sweet life I just left.

As I fish in my pocket for coins to buy an English newspaper, I feel sure that interior silence is possible to maintain in the city, just not by me.

The bus I board that carries me to the airport holds only a few other passengers. Finding an empty row of seats, I spread the newspaper open to catch up on what I've missed. No surprises. The rich are still rich, the powerful are still in power, and my sports teams are still mediocre. These linear doses of information I wanted to regard in a whole, fresh way—with eyes pure and a soul sharpened by Valaam so that I would see only the good in all things. I wanted my reacquaintance with the world to be like seeing an old friend in a new light after we both had done something transforming. But as we turn from the curb, these mostly trivial reports leave me feeling anchored uncomfortably to this world.

After a brief but troubled negotiation with Russian customs officials, thankfully not as alarming as my entry into this country, I climb aboard an airplane heading west toward Helsinki. No wonder the officials were contentious: I look awful. The dirt clinging to my clothing is practically an additional piece of luggage. And from head to toe I resemble a vagabond who has never found a body of water in which to bathe. The water of Lake Ladoga was so cold that I could manage only a few dips in three weeks. I notice, too, that my weight loss has thinned the skin on my face. But what I lose in fashion, I gain in freedom. I settle into my seat and into a pleasant calm. Fresh from five weeks of poignant experiences, I become happily oblivious of the swirling activity of passengers around me.

Such a beautiful gift is this plane ride. Within an hour into the trip, all the small things—the peanuts and juice, the attendants walking the aisles, the white noise of the engines, the small windows, passengers turning pages, an Asian child to my left—wash together to send a gentle message that the transition from Valaam to America is underway, and that I needn't be anxious about it. With the traveling, a total of eight days will have passed between my last chapel service on the island and my arrival in Florida to meet my family. This eight-day passage is an important time, for, as one monk describes it, "when you leave Stillness, leave it slowly. Otherwise, you will tear your soul like fabric being ripped in two." A different kind of reflection is at hand. While at Valaam, I was immersed in experience; now, I consider the life to which I'm returning. How they will interact is one giant mystery.

Some of the best advice I've received recently about living in time has come from the Russian writer Leo Tolstoy. His story called "Three Questions" comes to mind as I swing wildly between the life to come and the life behind. Tolstoy writes of a king who wrestles with a riddle in the form of three questions—What is the most important time? Who is the most important person? and, Which is the most important task?

The king is a consummate opportunist, and is interested not in spirituality, but in strategy. At last he meets a hermit whose simple wisdom—simple, but smart and piercing—exposes the king to a new way of seeing the world: *Now* is the most important time; *Whoever is directly before me* is the most important person; *Whatever task I am presently engaged in* is the most important task. Tolstoy fleshed out in fiction what St. Paul preached in epistle: "Behold, now *is* the accepted time; behold, now *is* the day of salvation" (2 Corinthians 6:2). With the past having too many regrets, and the future too many questions, the burden of today—of this present moment—is sufficient. And, I discover, not unbearable.

We are one hour from Helsinki, and I enter into the joy of the moment. Even with the steady din of burning engine and rushing wind, a strong quiet fills the fuselage. Or maybe it fills my body. But I'll remember this: The devil says "yesterday or tomorrow"; the Holy Spirit says "today!"

Of course, what I discover as I hush the past and the future is that I'm painfully hungry in the present. A four-hour layover in the airport means I get to enjoy a wildly indulgent meal that would shame any self-controlled monastic. While at Valaam, our food was simple fare. We ate what the earth offered, and learned from wise men the unfortunate connection between a full stomach and a roving passion. Food was for survival and for strength in accomplishing the important tasks germane to piety. Soon after my arrival in Helsinki, I am reminded just how creative we humans have become in pleasing the tongue. Yes, I should exercise discipline and take only what I need. But unhindered by such virtue, I start the hunt.

The wares of the world intensify to a fervent pitch as I take in the sights and smells of a dozen cuisines. Suddenly, the choice becomes clear. Above all other offerings, one emerges; silencing the cacophony, one beautiful siren; bringing order and sense to my world, one perfect item gently draws me near, laying to rest all other suitors. There, framed lovingly by the window of a gift shop, is chocolate. Weeks of only beans and bread does something to a man. It may strip him of his need for sweets, but not his desire.

With an act of abandonment of which I should be heartily ashamed, I breeze through the shop doors—probably knocking over an old woman or two—and come to rest before a wall of shelves covered with the finest gourmet chocolate known to man. I have worshipped at this altar before; it runs in my family.

The shiny and colorful packages are bested only by what I know hides inside them. Without quibbling over quality or ingredients, I lunge forward to sweep what may have been an entire line of chocolate products off the shelf and into my arms. It is quite possible that I single-handedly saved a candy company from financial collapse by that one motion. If I hadn't exercised at least a fragment of decency, I would have ignored the pesky little requirement of having to buy an item before using it. There, sprawled on the floor, I would have ripped the wrappings from those glorious bars and hurled them into my body without stopping to bite, taste, or chew. And with a face covered in chocolate stains, I would have strolled to the counter carrying only the shreds of a few hundred wrappers and said, "Here, charge me for what these used to be."

Instead, a cooler head prevails. I wait until I purchase the chocolate bars before consuming them. Satisfied, I wander the airport sampling other foods and reading magazines. My first encounter in weeks with the global cafeteria of information, products, and services, and I easily shed the self-restraint I learned from living at a monastery. Still, I carry no guilt. This is a crazy world and full of dangerous distractions, to be sure, but I am only eager to discover what may become a new world for me: a world where people and things I used to dismiss, I now see as valuable and redeemable. A place where I discern the Holy Spirit, "who," as the Orthodox pray, "is everywhere present and fills all things."

Having scoured the shops and corners of the Helsinki airport, I hear my call to board the plane to America. A rush of relief is like wind at my back; I'm ready to go home. Yes, the oil-and-water tension of Valaam and America adds a sublime bitterness to the taste of the moment, but I'm eager to see my family and friends. And to rest. With the dizzying slate of experiences at Valaam came a heightened sense of awareness, of expectation, but also a fatigue from forcing my senses to stay sharp for weeks. At least when I'm home, I can hide for awhile behind what is familiar and easy. Too, I can sleep in.

We rise and level. The vast, dark blueness of the Atlantic below will be the only scenery available for hours. So now the real work begins. What has been mere encounter must soon become habit. What is clear to me now, though, is the futility of simply trying to reproduce Valaam on American soil. It won't work. It would fail just as have the efforts to strictly copy the "early Church" and make it static forever.

If Christ is alive, then He is available to every culture in every time in every place. Valaam Monastery, then, will take root in American soil if it first takes root in the hearts of those who encounter it. As persons are converted, so are cultures. I imagine the numberless Americans who have had a genuine encounter with the Divine, and who are, in some way, transformed because of it. God is a fountain whose water purifies and flows without pause. That water of Eden can soften hearts and moisten the soil of even the driest and most arid land.

POVERTY

Monasteries are homes to men and women who devote a lifetime to keeping promises. When a monk enters the monastic community, he agrees to lay aside his former techniques for securing his salvation—also laying aside his definitions of what he understood to be spiritual success—and vows to follow the ancient path marked by poverty, chastity, obedience, and stability. These qualities are not emphatically distinct, but are intertwined into a life devoted to God and detached from this world.

The vow is made to God, under the abbot, and within the brotherhood. His life as a monk is one of waking up every morning and renewing his commitment to that vow. His renewal is not done in isolation, but under the guidance of an experienced spiritual director. One desert father notes the hazard of self-governance this way: "He who has himself for a spiritual father, has a fool."

Dawn breaks on my first day back in America. I feel a palpable longing to live now in accordance with the standard I witnessed on the island of Valaam Monastery. Not to live as a monk, of course, but with greater care for life's details. God's grace drew me to that place, and His grace is sufficient to draw that place back to me. Valaam is the structure, the

127

principle that dwells just beyond my field of vision, enlivening conscience and imagination.

It has been less than two months since I left America, but it feels as if I have been away for years. What colors most of what I do now is a vague annoyance that comes from knowing a place while feeling completely foreign to it. I make no presumption to know perfectly how to assimilate that island with this nation, that culture with this culture. That critical work will happen in what I assume will be an appropriate passage of time. For now, patience is a priority.

Principal among my tasks is to rest and evaluate. But on my first evening home, Valaam makes a surprising appearance. Before the pilgrimage, my morning or evening prayer time was spent sitting down. Being seated wasn't a statement or a technique, it was simply a position of comfort. The prayer cycle at Valaam, however, was infused with calls to be attentive. We didn't sit for most of the time we prayed; we stood. Standing sharpened my mind and brought a necessary sobriety to the act of praying. Tonight, then, I face the icons and stand to pray.

The days unfold with other small and subtle revolutions in thought and behavior. An innocuous trip to the grocery store ends in empathy for the hundreds of people who will walk saturated and numbed through its aisles of abundance. Our problem isn't a lack of convenience, but a lack of contentment. And while it is easy and nice and pleasurable to have more than one option to meet a need or satisfy a desire, a danger lurks of becoming people who lust. We become gluttonous in desire, implacable in demand. I survey the huge selection of food, for example, and notice that my hunger grows equally selective about what will satisfy it.

On my way home from the store, I remember the food at

Valaam. Some of it was beyond terrible; most, not palatable to a finicky tongue raised on bounty. But mealtime evolved into something precious in its simplicity. To know what we would receive, and that the portions were sufficient to satisfy the needs of the body, somehow made us less self-centered. Our attention shifted to the natural beauty of the island, to the rich conversation of fellow pilgrims, or, when we dined with the monks, to the lessons learned from eating in silence.

We were discovering an elusive pleasure of poverty. The playwright Moliére describes such an individual as one who "eats to live, not lives to eat." Then, on the occasion of a feast day at the monastery, when the salads and jams we had lived without were made available, we learned that common fare could hold surprising delight. It was a discovery made as a result not of feasting, but of fasting.

The monastic practice of poverty is not limited to food, or even economics. It is a testament to how addicted to money our culture has become that we think of poverty primarily in economic terms. To be sure, the monastic vow of poverty does include a turning from both wealth and the pursuit of it. But poverty means something greater than having only a few coins to rub together. It can also be defined as "nonpossessiveness." Monastic poverty is a fundamental agreement with God to follow Him unencumbered and without pause. The man with nothing follows God nimbly; the man with everything hesitates and evaluates what he might lose by doing so.

St. John Climacus—a sixth-century monk who lived on Mt. Sinai—comments on this physical and spiritual lightness in his work, *The Ladder of Divine Ascent.* He describes nonpossessiveness as "the resignation of cares, life without anxiety, an unencumbered wayfaring, alienation from sorrow, and fidelity to the commandments."[7] This earthly physician of the soul sees our *attachment* to aspirations, to ideas, to self, to the materials and matters with which we surround ourselves, as a fundamental cause of psychological and spiritual conflict. And it is precisely this attachment, this possessiveness, that clouds our vision and risks neglecting what God wants us to do and to have.

Is it possible to *have* and not to be attached? Can one acquire wealth and material abundance without being possessed by them? Christ never says the rich cannot be saved, just that it is "easier for a camel to go through the eye of a needle than for a rich man to enter the kingdom of God" (Matthew 19:24; Mark 10:25; Luke 18:25). For many of us, it may be as simple as the Law of Accessibility—what is most accessible is most covetable. Our hands reach for those things closest to them, and appetite may grow in proportion to abundance.

Key to understanding our proclivity toward possessiveness is an honest admission of the unknowability of the heart. Simply, we are not as strong as we think we are. Nor are we as trustworthy. The practice of poverty shares space with the virtue of humility. Without humility, poverty ceases to be a deposit of virtue. Certainly, temptations lurk in lack as well as in abundance. A man can grow proud of all he doesn't have, and all that he can live without.

I move through my first days back in America with clumsy applications of the practice of poverty. Without possessing much maturity to discern whether my attempts are worthwhile, I occasionally try the obvious: eating one dessert instead of two; turning from tempting advertisements; settling for older clothing when I have the money to purchase newer. Old habits are difficult to supplant. And I sigh at how easily I forget Valaam in the swamp of unlimited opportunities to pamper and indulge.

A dim uneasiness moves with me. I've never been adept at self-denial anyway, but I am beginning to wonder if the practice of poverty is only a state of living without much of anything. Is it a constant practice of neglecting? of avoiding? Does the will grow stronger with this kind of negative exercise until eventually I desire nothing, choose nothing, see "meaning" in nothing? That life seems as if it is not life. That, I remember, was the logical destination for my interest in Buddhism—detachment to the point of becoming a corpse.

The uneasiness shifts to a new longing. To be nonpossessive without being attached to *something,* I reason, must be like fasting from food without feasting on prayer. To only do without won't do. Gradually, mercifully, another dimension of the practice of poverty emerges. The Orthodox Faith rests on the foundation of the Holy Trinity. To worship the God who is the "I Am," the Son in whom "dwells all the fullness of the Godhead" (Colossians 2:9), and the Holy Spirit who is "everywhere present and fills all things," is to worship in a space not of empty absence, but of pure Presence!

What I could vaguely imagine as theory is concretely explained in print. *The Ladder of Divine Ascent* offers this insight: "He who has tasted the things on high easily despises what is below, but he who has not tasted the things above finds joy in possessions."[8] An authentic, Christian state of nonpossessiveness requires an *experience* with the abundance of the Kingdom of God. The practice of Christian poverty, then, is ultimately a positive condition; it is a condition of living without so that we have room for what is heavenly. It is a state full of anticipation.

It is also a state full of pain. Spiritual and material poverty as a way of life requires the denial of self. In the program taught by Christ—indeed, exemplified by Him—self-denial is an act that includes taking up our cross. We will find ourselves following Christ into the Garden of Gethsemane, pleading for relief or dismissal of the burden before us, only to relinquish our will so that God's will may be done. Then we follow Him to His cross.

One evening, while leaning against the old and scuffed southern outside wall of the room used as an infirmary at Valaam, I listened to a monk share how he learned of the monastic life. He spoke limited English in broken phrases and frustrated gestures. He explained that he first joined a monastery in St. Petersburg. When he entered, he was directed by that monastery's abbot to bring with him only what he could carry on his back or in his pocket. What followed was a long, agonizing struggle over a family photograph.

This middle-aged man wore sharp eyes over a full and wild beard. He had a body language always one step behind his active mind. While in the world, rock music was his occupation, and he alluded to it as if some of the more painful memories were still fresh. He moved to Valaam after an undisclosed period of time in St. Petersburg. For this man, the monastic way meant shedding the cares of his former life.

Even as fresh as his former life remained, leaving most of his possessions was not difficult. But one item he ached to carry with him as he crossed the threshold from pagan to pilgrim was a photograph of his parents and three siblings. This man referred to his struggle whether to keep this photograph when he entered the monastic life as "a time of craziness." From his speech and his behavior, it was clear that the memories and emotions that accompanied his photograph were too large to carry on his back or in his pocket. He left the photograph behind.

It is a principle that we who aren't monastics find difficult to understand. We who rely mostly on habit to categorize attachments as good and bad, as worth keeping or worth leaving, look quizzically on this man with his small and innocent photograph. It's a perfectly good item, we assume. But to him who was entering a life of fierce single-mindedness of focus on God, it was a possession. And the problem was that it possessed him.

Later that evening, I strolled through the living quarters of other monks, and noticed that they too kept few "relics" of their past. Each no larger than a bedroom, the dwellings contained small beds and beige walls often colored with a spectacular variety of icons, crosses, candles, and simple items—a dried flower, a ribbon—that held a story known only by him who lived there.

What was noticeably absent was evidence of the life he left behind.

Since the vow of obedience is common to all monks, yet often specific in its application, one monk may be allowed to possess what another monk isn't. Both, though, are required to take seriously Christ's words, recorded by St. Matthew as a warning against any competing allegiances: "He who loves his father or mother more than Me is not worthy of Me. And he who loves son or daughter more than Me is not worthy of Me" (Matthew 10:37). This statement is just prior to one where the Lord declares unworthy him "who does not take his cross and follow after Me" (10:38). Yes, that cross: it is one possession of which we are to take firm hold.

The last verse in this trilogy of sobering statements burns the fog from our eyes, enabling us to see that the way of Christian poverty is the way—indeed, the only way—to abundant life. "He who finds his life," Jesus says, "will lose it, and he who loses his life for My sake will find it" (Matthew 10:39).

All creation groans for the fulfillment and resolution found in Christ. We are part of that creation, and our longing will be satisfied only by shedding the substitutes and acquiring Christ.

I have experienced brief, rare moments when, after receiving Holy Communion, everything before my eyes seemed to burst with deeper and richer color. As I stepped outside, there were trees and plants I didn't remember appearing so bright and alive. This clarity belongs to Christ; it is His quality, not ours. We come with arms emptied of attachment, of possessiveness, to receive that which only He can give—our true life.

That divine exchange of losing and finding life is practiced as we move among those who are in true need. The monks at Valaam live without possessions partly to support a small community of peasants who live around the monastery. It's an organic relationship: poverty and charity. To choose nonpossessiveness is a way to love the neighbor who is poor not by choice but by circumstance. The food not consumed during Great Lent, for example, is to be given to those who don't eat because they have no other option.

As the days of my reacquaintance with America unfold, poverty is the monastic vow I find easiest to reflect upon. No shortage exists of temptations to be possessive. A congestion of shops and stores is minutes from where I live, and the urge prompts commercial grazing. Before that, though, I confront the pesky assumption that I will drive, not walk. Ease of selection, ease of purchase, ease of access. I put more effort into pouring milk on cereal.

But I am blessed. A shining example of the practice of poverty lives under the very roof over my head. My grandmother moves through life in a way that favors the abundance of the soul over the bounty of society. And her starting point for this way of life, her lens through which she sees her place in the world, is the first Beatitude: Blessed are the poor in spirit, for theirs is the Kingdom of heaven.

Gram grasps this purest definition of poverty as offered by our Lord. To make a vow of nonpossessiveness as a Christian is to confess, first and foremost, our poverty before the throne of God. Much of the strength of her life, and of her witness, is found in her humble pleading for more of God's provision, more of His love, in whatever way He chooses to manifest those riches in her life. Her practice, like mine, is personal. No easy formula for what to sacrifice and what to possess seems to exist; the depth and character of an individual's practice of poverty is an ongoing series of decisions performed with the counsel of the wise.

In Gram, I see one who walks in communion with God. She is conscious of her faults and has no greater or fewer than any other aged and godly woman. But the word "mercy" is never far from her conversation. Gram believes that she is most in need of mercy; therefore she has only mercy to give.

In his book, *The Ladder of the Beatitudes,* Jim Forest offers a series of perceptive thoughts on what it means to be "poor in spirit." If free, the imagination can draw a dozen quick relationships between the condition of the soul described, and what should be the behavior of him who possesses such a soul:

> What does poverty of spirit mean? It is my awareness that I cannot save myself, that I am basically defenseless, that neither money nor power will spare me from suffering and death, and that no matter what I achieve and acquire in this life, it will be far less than what I wanted. Poverty of spirit is my awareness that I need God's help and mercy more than I need anything else.

Poverty of spirit is getting free of the rule of fear, fear being the great force that restrains us from acts of love. Being poor in spirit means letting go of the myth that the more I possess, the happier I'll be. It is an outlook summed up in a French proverb: When you die, you carry in your clutched hand only what you gave away.[9]

"Poverty of spirit," he continues, "is a letting go of self and of all that keeps you locked in yourself." The possessive man is distinguishable by the castle and moat that hide his love. He is not a free man. He is skilled at the art of separation, of isolation. In contrast, the monastic life is a slow, steady, determined effort to fill the moat and tear down the castle. In my first days back in America, I survey the landscape of my country and of my soul, and see empires.

CHAPTER 14

CHASTITY

"The Christian ideal has not been tried and found wanting;" commented G. K. Chesterton in his ambitiously titled book, *What's Wrong with the World*, "it has been found difficult and left untried." [10] Of all the places where such a quotation would come to mind, I am surprised to find among them this southwestern Florida beach.

But it's a natural thought, really. As natural for a religious man in this environment as thoughts of freedom are to a man in prison. An ideal lingers in the mind, and proof of its elusiveness is found no farther than in the walls of habit and circumstance that seem insurmountable. In this sea of sun-worshippers, with hundreds of sculptures parading slowly over the sands patched with just enough fabric to avoid arrest, that ideal is chastity.

As with poverty and economics, so with chastity and sexuality: our consideration of virtue is often limited to the obvious. Instead, the monastic practice of poverty reaches deep into the soul to free a man of addiction and possessiveness; and the practice of chastity reaches deep into the mind to make a man whole again. Chastity is not limited to sexuality, but that's where we assume it belongs.

Chastity defined? One passage from *Great Lent,* by Father

Alexander Schmemann, explains chastity to be a positive virtue that reaches the whole of a person:

> Chastity! If one does not reduce this term, as is so often and erroneously done, only to its sexual connotations, it is understood as the positive counterpart of sloth. The exact and full translation . . . ought to be *whole-mindedness.* Sloth is, first of all, dissipation, the brokenness of our vision and energy, the inability to see the whole. Its opposite then is precisely *wholeness.* If we usually mean by chastity the virtue opposed to sexual depravity, it is because the broken character of our existence is nowhere better manifested than in sexual lust—the alienation of the body from the life and control of the spirit.[11]

The chaste man, in Fr. Alexander's explanation, is identifiable by his sturdy integrity. His health as a sexually chaste being may reach into other areas of his life, so that his "vision and energy" are in line with his deepest principles. But a man who has for a principle the violation of chastity may be identifiable by his deep conflict. And that would make sense: Christ came to save not portions of a man, but the whole of him. What we withhold will work against what we give, resulting in disintegration. To yield to God something less than everything is ultimately to court madness.

But what about the world? Satisfying the secular gospel on the matter of chastity means that one must simply engage in "selective promiscuity." Get through life without contracting some dreaded disease; try to practice monogamy; stay married for a lifetime if you can; almost never cheat. Do these, the culture tells us, and you're a candidate for sainthood.

But here on the beach there exists an obvious tension: the demands of the Christian life are as severe as the degrees we will go to avoid them. Our Lord says: "You have heard that it was said to those of old, 'You shall not commit adultery.' But I say to you that whoever looks at a woman to lust for her has already committed adultery with her in his heart" (Matthew 5:27–28). And it is precisely the heart that is in need of the care and attention given instead to the bodies on display. But we are too skilled in ignoring our desperate condition. It is as if Jesus is walking amid this carnival of desire, offering a cure to the brokenness that none of us, numbed by our revelry, really feels.

On the drive home, dusk taints the distant edge of a blue sky. I feel the conviction of violating both the virtue of chastity, for I have divorced my faith from my carnal appetite, and the practice of poverty, for I have coveted. Of course, it makes clear sense now why a monk does not live in a condominium on the beach. Those high concrete walls at Valaam are meant as much to keep virtue in as to keep intruders out.

The men there, endowed with no less energy or sexual drive than others, are striving not to quench their youthful passion but to cast off the fuels that enflame it. Passion, in Orthodox life, is a good thing. It is a part of human nature that, when channeled in proper service to God, changes fear into courage and sinners into saints. If not cleansed, it can destroy.

The monastic life is a high calling and conducive to the acquisition of chastity. It is a physical and spiritual progression toward the healing of the whole person. Also, it is a condition where one's fiercest battles are often fought in the imagination, so strict accountability to a spiritual director is crucial (one struggle specific to the monk is the continual *acceptance* of the single life to which he has committed himself).

Since I have neither the calling nor the concentration to be a monk, I inquire of a priest for advice on chastity. His reply? Singular devotion to the local parish. Every Orthodox Christian is expected to attend the services. In fact, we find a sobering mandate in a church canon that he who misses the celebration of Holy Communion more than twice consecutively, excommunicates himself. Reconciliation with the Church is undertaken through the sacrament of confession and a good talk with the priest. To attend the services, though, is to encounter the communion of the saints, that "great cloud of witnesses" (Hebrews 12:1) present, worshiping, surrounding.

Devotion to one's local church also builds friendships. But what nurtures the health and wholeness of a person is that one's social life revolves around the services of the church, rather than the church revolving around one's life. What binds the horizontal relationships, then, is a decidedly vertical focus. As I have surveyed the literature on communes, and have even moved lightly in those circles, I have discovered that, at least for me, there can be no community without communion, and there can be no communion without Christ.

A heart that is chaste will see not only friends as divine, but strangers, too. This, sadly, is an experience I have not had with much consistency. When confronted with the unfamiliar, my posture often becomes distant or defensive. But there is another way, exemplified by the beautiful experience described by Thomas Merton, the twentieth-century Trappist monk.

Merton recounts in his journal, *A Search for Solitude,* that he tasted the fruit of his devotion to chastity in what he refers to as his "Fourth and Walnut Epiphany" of March 18, 1958.

Standing on a street corner, he suddenly began to take special notice of the people around him. And in that sea of strangers, he saw the divinely familiar. Especially about the women pedestrians, he observed:

> I am keenly conscious, not of their beauty (I hardly think I saw anyone really beautiful by special standards), but of their humanity, their womanness. But what incomprehensible beauty is there, what secret beauty that would perhaps be inaccessible to me if I were not dedicated to a different way of life.

Merton suggests that to experience wholeness, one must necessarily reject brokenness. To repent of all that contributes to one's fragmentation of soul and personality is to obtain clarity, and to finally see the world of beauty that lies just behind the world of decay:

> It is as though by chastity I had come to be unafraid of what is most pure in all the women of the world, and to taste and sense the secret beauty in their girls' hearts as they walked in the sunlight—each one secret and good and lovely in the sight of God . . . as good as and even more beautiful than life itself. For the womanness that is in each of them is at once original and inexhaustibly fruitful, bringing the image of God into the world.[12]

There it is: a vision of wholeness granted to him who strives to clean and mend the lenses through which he sees the world. Then, the fragmentation of body from soul, physical from spiritual, us from God, fades. But the abundance of God's blessing isn't stilled with simply seeing more of the internal beauty of those around us. We begin to see Wisdom. The divine thread that holds all things together, the love unspeakable that lay for so long just beyond our senses, the mystery of the ordinary, that is what we begin to see. And it is more than a vision, it is a way of life.

But it is not my life. The books about saints who have acquired this life of wholeness surround me like photographs of some distant land. They lie two and three high beside the local newspaper and a calendar of cultural events. A ticket stub from a movie theater marks my place in one of them. They share a bedside table with a television remote control. Fresh from the monastery, I do not yet possess sensibilities sharp enough to determine what of my culture to engage and enjoy and what to reject and avoid.

The books tell me that chastity heals the mind. The chaste man—the whole man—is he who possesses the discernment necessary to detect the brokenness around him, and especially when he is in danger of being broken by it. St. James, the brother of our Lord, observes that the double-minded man is "unstable in all his ways" (James 1:8). But the whole man leans toward stability, braced through the waves of temptation.

One indication of the brokenness of our culture is the place that pleasure enjoys in it. Pleasure is deified. Not just sexual satisfaction, but pleasure as a thick coating on the whole of life, worthy of maniacal pursuit. The motivation behind much of our behavior is either to maximize pleasure or to minimize pain. And because pleasure and pain are our primary preoccupations, we miss our greater purpose of the balanced wholeness to which these, with a host of other human experiences, point.

As I survey the contours of our cultural landscape, I absorb many shades of divine beauty. Even beyond the natural wonders unique to her place on earth, America offers occasional treasures in literature, in medicine, in art and music. And though it is heavily abused, the liberty we enjoy is the envy of distant millions who live daily under any number of oppressions that reach us only as newspaper headlines.

No culture, then, is thoroughly corrupt, because no culture exists outside of the Holy Spirit, who "is everywhere present and fills all things." But America certainly seems committed to declaring its independence. The pleasures of "the world, the flesh, and the devil" spill from our televisions, our magazines, our billboards and boardrooms. These are not the pleasures that originate from a redeemed heart, but from a sinful one, and to a sinful heart do they appeal.

To throw a blanket of condemnation over all cultural pleasures—pure or base—is, I believe, not the task. More important is *discernment*. To possess wisdom; to know when to enjoy; to know what is tempting me toward ruin and when I am in danger of relenting; to understand how my relationship with pleasure affects me and my relationships; to sense when human dignity is encouraged or assaulted; to know when it is proper to dance and celebrate, or to hesitate and avoid; to hear the voice of God about the world around me, inviting or cautioning; all this is the reward of holy discernment. And discernment is the better part of chastity.

The chaste man, then, is not a somber or morbid man. He is a free man. With control over his passions, he pours himself into those celebrations that are life-affirming and not soul-destroying. His mirth is hearty and healthy. His chastity has wiped the dirt from his windows and revealed to him the purer pleasures that are like blossoms of the abundant life given to us by Jesus. This is the natural way; it is we who have become unnatural.

Night has fallen thoroughly as I pass the houses in my neighborhood. So much goodness rests on earth, but it feels hidden. Most of these homes are dimly lit by television screens. From those screens come evening news programs with their litany of sad events and sadder explanations. They act as if they have no choice but to draw our attention away from the deeper issue that dwells below the rotting surface: Our crisis is not sociological, it is theological. Forsake God and life becomes god-forsaken. Indeed, one will learn quickly that hell is real if he lives as if heaven is not.

I speak briefly with Gram as I walk through the door. She's watching television too, but it appears to be a program about gospel music. As I pass her room, I remember her telling me that life with God is "an everyday walk." She feels more spiritually vulnerable in her late age than ever before; I'm not sure why. But I've heard that the life of holiness is a battle unto the last beat of the heart.

Like other virtues, then, chastity must be a practice of perseverance. St. John Climacus speaks to this prolonged effort. Tonight, I open *The Ladder of Divine Ascent* and discover that chastity is a treasure that can be snatched from us at any time, at any stage:

> With beginners, falls from chastity usually occur by reason of luxury; with intermediates, because of haughtiness as well as from the same cause which leads to the fall of beginners; and with those approaching perfection, solely from judging their neighbor.[13]

I lay the book on my lap and rub my eyes. The sun at the beach has made the skin on my face tender. Behind closed eyes, my mind wanders to Valaam again—not an infrequent trip these days. At one time I may have been among those who criticize monastic seclusion as a fleeing from the "real battles" of the world. Now I know better: Those men and women are warriors. In fact, to *refrain* from engaging culture is, for some, evidence of chastity.

Like that sun set high, virtue seems lofty and out of reach. I speak of it easily in sweeping and florid language, using rich adjectives but, because of my inexperience, few verbs. Thankfully, to this tendency comes the cold reality of sainthood. There have lived men and women of true and real faithfulness. They have loved God above all and can speak of the glories and sufferings of that life forcefully and without embellishment.

As I open my eyes, the book before me seems too heavy, too intense. It's time to move on. There is a definite clue as to when I've had as much spiritual prose as I can handle in one sitting: I start assuming I understand what the author is writing about. Then, I start skimming. So it seems sensible to turn to stories then. Usually, it's less work. Tonight I choose a copy of *Lives of the Saints* as kindling for a sweet dream.

Instead, I find a story that leaves me sweetly shaken. Chastity, as revealed in the lives of the chaste, is no trivial acquisition. Many holy figures attached such import to the virtue that they gave their lives to preserve it within themselves. From the class of saints known as "virgin-martyrs," there is the account of St. Euphrasia of Nicomedia.

St. Euphrasia was born into a wealthy family. Her environment was the third-century town of Nicomedia—a place then under the harsh anti-Christian rule of Emperor Maximian. Her reputation as a woman of wisdom and Christian devotion spread as the acts of charity she humbly tried to conceal became public. In an effort to crush this holy woman and her influence, the authorities arrested her and tried vigorously to coerce her to renounce her faith in Christ and to sacrifice to idols.

Although beaten severely, Euphrasia remained resolute. The authorities regrouped. A new strategy was drafted, designed to attack the one virtue she held most dear—her virginity. For Euphrasia, chastity was a way of life, with virginity being its quiet evidence. Delivered into the ravenous hands of a barbarian with the purpose of defiling her, Euphrasia prayed that God would grant her wisdom in this difficult circumstance and preservation of this precious virtue.

With her adversary, she struck a clever deal. If he would not violate her, she could offer a special potion that would render him invincible in warfare. Drink it, she instructed, and no sword could harm him. As proof of the potion's effectiveness, she persuaded him to experiment on her own neck. After taking some of the potion, she stretched forward. The barbarian swung his sword and Euphrasia's head fell to the ground.

CHAPTER 15

OBEDIENCE

Martyrdom—I'll risk the obvious—requires the whole of a life. It is a twisted compliment from the executioner that he takes your faith seriously enough to kill you for it. The practice of complete devotion shines a searing light into the darkness and onto those who dwell there. The barbarian and the powers behind him, because they did not get the depravity they craved, were ravenous not so much for the head of St. Euphrasia, but for the head of Christ.

We who have not yet been summoned to bodily martyrdom can still live a life of holy dying.

This dying, though, gives birth to abundant life. It is the way of obedience.

Obedience is two hands stretched toward heaven, into which other virtues are laid in return. We receive a greater yield than we give from Him who, as St. Paul notes, is "able to do exceedingly abundantly above all that we ask or think" (Ephesians 3:20). But even this favorable transaction is given no place in the selfish economy of our age of rugged individualism. To the man who obeys no creed but his own, obedience is unappealing.

And to an ego in rebellion, it is utterly toxic. Obedience

147

is, according to the Alexandrian Saint Syncletica, a "greater virtue than chastity, however perfect. Chastity carries within it the danger of pride, but obedience has within it the promise of humility."[14] And humility is precisely what this rebellious boy needs. Without it I will never honor the calling given to me by Elder Raphael.

A day before Elder Raphael came to our camp, I was clearing mud and moss from the north face of the small chapel on our island. The sky was clear and the sun close. In the afternoon, between lunch and dinner, our whole group enjoyed a break. I leaned against the high scaffolding and observed some pilgrims standing in the shade of a tree, some walking down the path toward the lake, and others huddled around the well. It was a relaxing and peaceful scene.

My respite activity was to retrieve a book from my tent and find a place to relax on the scaffolding. Positioning a few boards above me for shade, I lay down and placed my bundled shirt under my head for comfort. I had lost my place in a biography of the beloved Russian Saint Seraphim of Sarov, but settled for a rough approximation.

His biographer wrote with such admiration that I wondered if St. Seraphim's life could be adequately contained in mere words and paper. He is a saint who has influenced thousands. But the narrative flow of beautiful experiences was blunted by one event that I simply thought impossible. Famous is St. Seraphim's thousand-day *podvig* of prayer while kneeling on a rock. That, I thought, was believable, especially for an ascetic warrior like Seraphim. But his biographer recounted another story that cut to the heart of something that, at the time, troubled me about Orthodoxy.

While in church one day, St. Seraphim stood before an icon and engaged in a four-hour conversation with Mary, the

Theotokos, or "Birthgiver of God." His face, his whole demeanor, as others in attendance observed, was transfixed. So powerful was his experience that his slack body had to be carried to a seat. To a mind raised on religious but saintless education, this was baffling. I laid the book aside in a frustration born more of yearning than disgust. Is this possible? What happened to him? Why is his experience so far from mine? Mary is an important figure in the Gospels, I assented, and I know she is venerated by us Orthodox. But a four-hour talk? These thoughts ran like cold threads through the story.

In an impetuous move, I grabbed my shirt and ambled down the scaffolding toward the chapel's old, dusty nave. Crossing the wood floor, I approached with boldness the icon of Mary. Our group had placed the icon on the wall to the left of the altar's royal doors, where her icons would have hung decades earlier. In a spirit of demand, I stood before her icon and quietly but resolutely poured my questions at her feet.

Who are you? Why don't I know you? Do you speak to God's people? Would you ever speak to me? Are you real? Falling from my tongue were pleas I had only uttered to one other figure years ago—Christ Himself. But there was no desperation here. My experience was one of possessing a deep sense of surrounding safety, where struggle and doubt were given room to breathe and to be confronted. It was like the Church itself, where one can twist and writhe within, and even against, a loving embrace that will always hold.

Time passed unnoticed. Even as my mouth fell silent, my heart churned with petitions and random thoughts about this woman before me. In the cool chapel, with sunlight forming shapes on the floor, something surprising happened. I didn't hear anyone, I didn't converse with anyone, and I certainly heard no one conversing with me. But suddenly, with a strength both delicate and definite, I started praying for my mother.

The transition from a focused intensity on Mary to a yearning for the healing and wholeness of my mother felt smooth and seamless. That, in itself, was surprising, since I didn't expect to meet anyone in this chapel except the Mother of Jesus. But as I drifted between prayer and being conscious of the strangeness of that prayer, I discovered that there was a deep rightness in this experience.

Nothing specific filled out the image of my mother in my mind, only that she was near. Like a flower on the surface of a river, she was placed into the current of prayer toward the Theotokos. I prayed for nothing in detail, only asking Mary to be with my mother, to pray to God for her. And in that simple supplication, there emerged a faint and distant stirring that Mary *is* a real person. She was chosen by the Lord and "all generations call her blessed" (Luke 1:48). It is possible, then, that the Mother of Jesus—she who gave birth to the Incarnate God, she who is pure woman, she who is our fullest expression of cooperation with the healing Holy Spirit—would know those secret places where women hurt. Where mothers hurt.

I stood before the icon while praying to Mary and felt absolutely no hint of treason. Christ was King. He was the Lord and God and Savior to whom all the prayers of all His people flow. His sovereignty and my salvation were not "threatened" by my supplications to Mary. Instead, I began to sense a new fullness to His power as the cosmic Christ of whom St. Paul wrote: "By Him all things were created. . . . He is before all things, and in Him all things consist" (Colossians 1:16, 17). The Queen of Heaven receives Her royalty from the King of all.

Outside a near chapel window I heard the dull scuffle of workboots on wood. Our break was over. I stood before the icon of Mary for a few moments longer. Turning toward the door, I understood that all great truths enter slowly into the soul, and, if nurtured, eventually make a difference. My visit here was brief, even subtle, but my mind had crossed a threshold. As I emerged from the chapel and into the light, I wondered how long it would be before I completely believed.

Zen has a proverb: After the ecstasy, the laundry. As the day passed, I didn't give much thought to my time before the icon. The work and chores of the day managed to ground me in tedium and temperance. When I did reflect briefly upon my time in the chapel, it felt more interesting than compelling. But the Zen proverb also means that the spiritual and physical dwell together. It was important to remember that the experience would remain an isolated event if I didn't remain open and inquisitive about it.

When the morning bell rang the following day, it was soon followed with the news that Elder Raphael would emerge from his simple home to visit us. He arrived by boat—Valaam's conventional transportation. Many in our group grew restless as Elder Raphael agreed to meet with us individually. He received us, with Deacon James interpreting, in the same chapel I had visited the day before.

One person at a time entered and emerged. Charming was the range of facial expressions as pilgrims left the elder's presence. Some walked from the chapel visibly wrestling with the words they had received; others simply smiled. One woman went straight for the forest and wasn't seen for hours. I entered the chapel and sat several feet from Elder Raphael and Deacon James.

I felt no fear.

In that peaceful place I began by telling Elder Raphael that I was glad he was here. Deacon James interpreted and the elder bowed his head and smiled widely, his clear eyes leaving mine for only a moment. In my hand was a piece of paper containing a few questions that sifted to the top of the heap that day. I also carried a pencil to record the elder's words. We moved through the questions unhurriedly, and the answers came through a high and quiet voice that pulled me forward. And as Deacon James translated from Russian to English, I listened and wrote carefully.

My last question was easy to ask because of its freshness—it had happened just the day before. I did not tell Elder Raphael anything about the experience with the icon of the Theotokos. The advice I needed was only about my loved one. "I have a burden for the salvation of my mother," I began. Deacon James translated, the head bowed. "And I don't know what to do. She has been on my mind lately and I believe she is in need of healing. Is there anything I can do?"

The translation took a few moments while Deacon James paused twice to find the right words. Then, without hesitation, Elder Raphael replied. The answer in English was smooth and sudden: "Pray to the Mother of God."

My pencil fluttered on the page but it couldn't have recorded my reaction, for it felt indescribable. I looked at Deacon James as if he were in on my secret, but I knew I was wonderfully alone. Elder Raphael continued: "Pray to the Theotokos one hundred and fifty times a day, and always remember to say, 'Lord, have mercy on my mother.'" I wrote in characters that I knew I would understand when I later referred to them: "Pray Mary, 150x." Our conversation was paced slowly and I had enough time to write each word, but I did not want to take my eyes off Elder Raphael.

With motion that must have seemed abrupt to the men in front of me, I stood and bowed in thankfulness. Elder Raphael lifted his hand and gave his blessing with the sign of the cross, then slid from his seat to his knees, lying prostrate before me. I, embarrassed by the blatant irony, fell in prostration before him. Each of the pilgrims with whom he met received the same farewell. If I had known a more appropriate sign of respect for this diminutive spiritual giant, I would have offered it freely.

I cannot imagine my facial expression when I emerged from the chapel. Those who stood nearby said nothing, either out of politeness or simply because they noticed nothing. With no work scheduled for the rest of the day, I could have gripped the paper in my hand and dashed for a secluded clearing on the other side of the island. Instead, I nervously poured a cup of tea by the fire and found a conversation to interrupt. We talked of sports and good-quality hiking boots. Camping stores were rated and each man told a tale about his favorite river back home.

After nightfall, I found Deacon James because I needed further explanation. What exactly did Elder Raphael mean when he said, "Pray to the Theotokos one hundred and fifty times a day"? Prayer I understood, but the quantity I didn't. Deacon James clarified that I am to say the prayer whose source is the Gospel according to St. Luke:

Rejoice, O Virgin Theotokos. Mary, full of grace, the Lord is with thee. Blessed art thou among women and blessed is the Fruit of thy womb, for thou hast borne the Savior of our souls.

I recorded the prayer on the same parchment that held the elder's earlier words. Oh, *that* prayer. The task suddenly grew intimidating. This was a long prayer, and I was to recite it one

hundred and fifty times daily without fail. Did I humbly rejoice in this blessing of sustained petition to the Great Lady
dwelling beside the throne of God? No. Measuring the task by
the effort required, I looked at the watch on my left wrist and
counted how many seconds passed as I uttered the prayer once.
Ten seconds died. Performing the math on the backs of my
eyelids, I figured that this duty, with the mandatory two yawns,
would absorb almost thirty minutes.

My tent that night was a cell of shame. Pure sloth, there.
The grumbling, though, was dismissed with amusement when
I reflected on the whole picture—the icon, my precious mother,
the astonishing gift of prayer. Obedience to a calling is not
easy, since it requires death to the contrary will. As sleep finally fell, I could only pray for the strength to pray.

Not long before I left Valaam to return home, I entered
the main church once more. Inside, in the small narthex separating the nave from the courtyard, an area against the wall is
devoted to selling worship items. Tourist and pilgrim alike
can purchase icons, candles, postcards, and books. It is a commercial operation that the monks find regrettable, but the
monastery is in steady need of money just to survive. From
this modest collection, I bought two icons of the Theotokos. I
carried them home to America as visual reminders of the obedience given to me by Elder Raphael.

Now, as I wander through the living room of the house
where I am staying, I pass the icons. They hang clearly within
sight. Beneath them is a small table that supports a prayer
book, a candle, and a prayer rope given to me by one of the
priests from Valaam. To have a sacred space is a new but precious quality of my life. Now, if I can just use it occasionally.

My obedience to Elder Raphael is but a taste of the perpetual obedience a monk practices with his spiritual father.

Big trouble can swirl in a young soul, and handling it often requires a measure of wisdom, patience, and hope that is difficult for the young to summon. The elder, who is farther along the spiritual path, can help by raising the young man's awareness of where temptations lurk, and by nurturing him in the ways of strength.

Should this practice of obedience occur within a traditional Christian context, with both novice and elder moving squarely within the Church's field of vision, the young man may even place his trust in the elder *instead* of in the larger framework of spirituality and ritual that the elder represents. This is not a simple development. A primary goal of obedience is to tame the will—often a higher priority than performing the rituals frequently or correctly.

From *The Sayings of the Desert Fathers,* one passage from an experienced guide offers this explanation:

> If someone has faith in another and hands himself over to him in complete submission . . . he can entrust his whole will to his father. He will suffer no reproach from God, for God looks for nothing from beginners so much as renunciation of the will through obedience.

Consider the farmer who works and reworks the soil until it is moist and tender enough to receive seed. If the purest kernels are tossed on hard and infertile ground, they are wasted and the harvest is lost. Obedience to a spiritual father, then, crumbles and prepares the heart. "A broken and a contrite heart," the Psalmist sings, "these, O God, You will not despise" (Psalm 51:17).

But as I wander through my first months back from the

monastery, even Elder Raphael's singular task proves challenging. I reason that thirty minutes of focused devotion out of sixteen waking hours isn't too much to ask. But it sometimes feels too much to give. I am faithful one day—standing before the icons, counting the repetitions with my fingers on the prayer rope, calling quietly with my lips for the intercession of the Theotokos to her Son—then negligent the next. The days of obedience bring confidence; failure brings penetrating guilt.

But then I remember: fall and get up, fall and get up, fall and get up. That is what the monk does and that is what I shall do—daily, hourly, for a lifetime. In the chapel, Elder Raphael could see the eternal while I could only see the immediate. He was imparting not just a task, but a way of life. And in the distance between that day on the island and this day in America, I have experienced growth I did not expect.

The memories of tension and loneliness in the house before my parents left each other no longer carry such sting; my small heart has grown to include the deepest yearnings for my mother to discover her true identity as a woman of God; I see our whole family in a fresh, graceful way; the Theotokos has become more dear; and, above all, the seed of God's love and sacrifice for His whole creation has found in me a slight but tender place to grow.

Abba Milos of Belos once said: "Obedience responds to obedience. When someone obeys God, then God obeys his request."[15] We see scriptural support for that. The Gospel according to St. John records Christ as saying, "Whatever you ask the Father in My name He will give you" (16:23). It is curious that the Prayer to the Theotokos carries within it no petition, only rejoicing and blessing. But even in those words, I am still pleading for her intercession: Help Mom. Hold her. Pray to God for her.

To obey without condition is pleasing in the sight of the Lord. But there are times when a hint of bargaining with God—I'll do this if You do that—slips into my prayers. Those times reveal an ugly selfishness, a concession to some kind of mock fatigue. They also uncover an inherent friction in the relationship of human and divine, where we are tempted either to assume our piety persuades God to perform our bidding, or to leverage our obedience in exchange for results.

Once again, the saints show another way. Not long ago, there lived on Mt. Athos a monk—Silouan—whose heart burned with love for the people of the world. His spiritual vision grew increasingly rich and clear as he struggled for salvation within the Athonite community. St. Silouan spoke highly of obedience, for it "preserves a man from pride." And obedience, suggests Silouan, "ranks above fasting and praying."

> The holy Fathers ranked obedience above fasting and prayer since a man who knows not obedience may think of himself as a spiritual wrestler and man of prayer, whereas he who has excised his self-will and put himself under obedience in all things to his elder and his confessor is serene in mind.[16]

Obedience, it seems, is a lifetime of effort. Even as temptations skirt the path before me, I will strive to be obedient to Elder Raphael. I will strive to stand before those icons and pray because it is the right thing to do, because I want to live well, but mostly because I love my mother. It is useless to wait until my soul is pure enough to pray with full hope and faith. I learned at Valaam to obey in body and the soul will follow. It may require a lifetime, but the soul will follow.

My family speaks openly about the soul. Each at least concedes that there exists a shadow of real behind the way things appear. Each refers to his or her personal library when in a season of searching. And when I wander into a fog, each kindly offers some direction.

In the end, though, our words might amount to ashes. To pray sincerely for the healing of her soul and body, to authenticate any hope for her wholeness, to effectively implore the Theotokos, not to insult God by the fluttering of my tongue toward heaven, I must do something else for my mother. I must live a worthy life.

The Epistle of St. James records that "the effective, fervent prayer of a righteous man avails much" (5:16). If I want my prayer to matter, then I must petition not just with my lips but with my life. My love for my mother—indeed, my love for anyone, and for the whole created order of the cosmos—is revealed in the way I live. Especially when no one is watching.

To intercede is to step into love's mystery. And when we intercede for someone near and familiar, who knows the personal details we keep hidden from others, we hope that our intercession is effective in spite of our open failures. We pray for our loved one to be ushered into a life of greater integrity, greater completeness and fullness than our lives have managed so far. With our pain, we stand praying in a sacred and humble place. The grace of God as the only saving power in this world becomes our focus, our deep desire as we fumble gloriously among family and friends.

CHAPTER 16

STABILITY

O nce, during an especially long and tedious service at the monastery, I settled my weary gaze on an old woman who had wandered in from the local village. She found her space among the cool tiles and tired bodies in the nave. My interest in her grew as hour upon hour unfolded languidly. Our pilgrimage group was participating—and here, one must stretch the definition of that word—in an all-night vigil.

Talk about rooted. The old woman stood for hours, with little movement other than to make the sign of the cross. Her still demeanor was an inspiring rebuke to my impatience. I brought my imagination to bear on this short, plump woman whose face lay hidden behind the folds of a dark and tattered scarf. Had she fallen asleep while standing? Not likely; she prostrated on cue. I imagined, rather, that from the soles of her feet grew thick and strong roots that twisted their way through the cement floor and into the deep, fibrous chambers of the earth.

If she was restless, it could only have been to search her heart for any corners she had yet to yield to God. So, perhaps restlessness and rootedness are not antithetical? Do I see in this cloaked figure that sacred tension of being *in* the world but not *of* it? From the details of her presence I created a story around her. Life in the wilderness and near the monastery had shaped her, like clay in the rugged but gentle hands of a potter. She appeared earthy and practical, while possessing a sensitivity to the holiness of the ground on which she stood. She loved both soil and spirit.

Our fine woman was practicing the art of stability. We have some like her here in America, especially among our elders. They are our unique examples of stability. It is not unusual to learn from one that he has lived all his days in the very house in which he was born, or in the same town. Or that he gave his sweat and energy to one craft or one vocation, and to one woman. He may have remained a faithful Christian, or met another god early in life and lived devotedly since: there is instruction in the steadfastness of his worship, even if his theology is different from our own. Often we learn that he knows about nature and sees himself as not entirely distinct from it. He may be finely tuned to the seasons, to the cycles of weather and harvest, because he has fixed himself in a position to observe the swirl of life around him. He is part of the swirl, but not part of the disquiet.

A stable man like this is like Job. We read in the Old Testament that God told Job to "speak to the earth, and it will teach you" (Job 12:8). Anyone who has attempted to learn the lessons of God through nature knows that His secrets there ooze forth like sap from a tree—slowly, inattentive to our demands. To observe, to listen, to grow aware of the glistening energy of life in the natural world nearby, this is the work and blessing of being still. And one must become still to become stable.

Stability as a monastic vow, as my dim eyes saw it practiced, seemed at first nothing more than staying in one monastery for a long time. Monks must fight their own version of consumer wanderlust: "If only I could live alone in that part of the forest"; "The monks are better at that monastery"; "If I could just get to the Holy Mountain, I could leave these amateurs behind." But as the days of my pilgrimage passed, I casually studied monastic literature—like *The Sayings of the Desert Fathers*—as a backdrop to what I was seeing, and a different picture began to form. True monastic stability involves not only living contentedly in every moment, but being constantly aware that everything one needs for his salvation resides in that precise moment in which he is living.

I carried this insight with me for a few days, marveling at how it seemed so simple, yet so slippery. Such contentment is surely a wellspring of freedom: the fierce grip of ambition must loosen as I accept my immediate circumstance as the means of my salvation. Mere acceptance, however, is unnatural to many. For some of us, unless we ache with hunger for achievement we aren't sure that we're alive. In our immediate circumstance, we often live with a feeling of being out of control. Staring into the future, we trip over the present.

The conditions for our contentment and awareness improve as we draw nearer to Christ. If an individual is called to the monastic life, that is where his cross and glory lie; if called to be married, there lie his cross and glory. To hear God's calling, one becomes still; to summon the obedience to that calling, one draws upon the Holy Spirit who takes root in stillness.

The contentment of stability also helps one look at his world with greater depth, confronting the horror and absorbing the beauty of what he sees. The divine energy that visited Moses and set the bush on fire without consuming it is the same energy that illuminates the cosmos—from fantastic mountains to fine matter. And it is the divine energy we find in us if it is given a chance to burn. The late poet Mary Guenevere Logan must have known something about the incandescence of creation, but also about the difficulty of discerning it, when she wrote:

> It is hard to always remember
> the God within us and among us,
> because He could not help but
> make a world of such distracting beauty,
> that we, inconstant
> darting hither and thither,
> trickle like raindrops on a pane of glass
> who find their crooked paths
> back to the solid earth.
> So we meander through the wonders
> of God, bedazzled, sure of
> the end, but full of forgetting.

I am beginning to discover these wonders of God. Settled again into a routine of life in America, new experiences are crowding the numerous memories I carried home from Valaam. I have been away from the monastery long enough to have weathered the grief of leaving it. A new ritual is emerging: strolling the beach at sunset, walking the cedar-chipped paths at a local park, turning my face and limbs toward the lifting wind, bending down to observe the explosion of color in a crocus. These are fledgling attempts to use motion to attain stability.

Americans are a migratory people. It is not unusual for us to travel from place to place—from birth to school to job to family to retirement to death. Our relationship with our environment of the moment is often cursory, marked more by how it makes us feel than how full of intrinsic richness and wonder it is. To discover that kind of nuance requires time and patience. Without an intimacy with our natural surrounding, we're more likely to treat it with suspicion or lack of interest, the way we might treat a stranger with whom we felt no connection.

I remember the drifting that characterized many of my college days. It was motion not as action, but as reaction—more fleeing than searching. Far from being spiritually productive, drifting of this kind leads to broken hearts and unfulfilled responsibilities. Our modern culture encourages this kind of motion. Shopping malls give us the selection to match, even train, our appetites; city streets are peppered with nightclubs that encourage "hopping" from one party to another; and even our religious landscape preaches the doctrine of convenience, where dissatisfaction with one church can send you browsing for another.

We might say that the journey of modern man is not vertical, but horizontal. His quest is not to discover the soul, but to be distracted from it. It is the sad migration made by him who lives in fear of all that lurks inside him, and of any silence that might bring it to surface. Modern man, to the degree that he is drunk on distraction and running from his shadow, is headed in the wrong direction. Modern man must move downward.

We must somehow learn to live among the locusts and honey and animal hair of our own interior wilderness, with St. John the Baptist as our guide. Some of what we will find on a pilgrimage through the soul is not attractive. But it may be good. Anger, sorrow, and fierceness may have a deeper relationship with love, joy, and peace than we understand.

Several weeks after I arrived home from the monastery, I

listened to a storyteller at a local library. She was reciting passages from the epics of ancient mythology. The wisdom found in those stories, she suggested, is timeless. Her accounts began with this prelude: "We are leaving our time now and honoring the five directions—north, south, east, west, and the vertical one that opens down into the soul." I like that. We are to honor not only the soul, but the journey that leads us to it. It is the journey of the spiritual man.

I am discovering that this journey, this kind of motion, leads to stability. And that this stability is not stagnation, but rootedness. The Christian language of sojourning—exile, exodus, pilgrimage, journey, walk with God—describes the linear, time-based traveling of God's people through this world. But it also suggests a vertical movement of discovering the Kingdom of God, which, our Lord says, is within us. It is a life of mostly internal adventure.

One saint who encountered such adventure in the life of another was Serapion. This fourth-century desert father loved to travel, but always distinguished between mere wandering and genuine pilgrimage. Word had reached him of a nun in Rome who had excelled in the spiritual life and who was a light of guidance for those around her. One quality of her life, however, confused him: she never left her small cell. Her ascetic life of sacrifice he understood; her devotion to daily prayer before her altar he admired. But for this nun to live all her days in the seclusion of her tiny dwelling, ostensibly neglecting the wonders of culture, was a curiosity for the restless Serapion.

One day, he approached her cell and paid a visit. With deference, Serapion inquired: "Why are you sitting here?" The holy woman turned and replied: "I am not sitting; I am on a journey."

We discover in these two figures two kinds of motion that are not incompatible. Serapion's physical journey was a symbol of the nun's spiritual journey, for both were seeking the holiness of the Kingdom of God. To believe in a Christ "in whom all things consist" is to recognize that as we travel through this world there are treasures everywhere—natural and cultural, obvious and hidden—that call our attention to Him who made them. And even when those treasures are soiled and broken, the very ache we feel is an indication that the pure, natural state of things has been violated.

Even the state of our relationships is affected by our vertical journey into the soul. To travel down authentically is an act of love toward others, for as one grows in personal grace he also grows in public mercy. Consider the cross—the base digs deep while the beams stretch wide to embrace the world to itself.

I am reminded again of the old woman from the village near Valaam, the one who stood rooted in the church among us restless American worshipers. The story I imagined from the details of her presence included friends and family who considered her piety one of the few reliable elements in their lives. Perhaps she stood there in the church representing the needs of those scattered souls for whom she felt a burden. She stood wearing their names before her Lord.

Many of us lament the condition of a loved one—that he is callous or that she is far from God. If we ourselves aren't callous and far, we have those in our lives who are. To attain a spirit of stability, of centeredness, in our lives is to leave a candle burning in the window for those who are lost and hungry and wandering through the night. "Acquire the spirit of peace," says the Russian Saint Seraphim of Sarov, "and a thousand souls around you will be saved."

Conversion often occurs when it seems least likely. The prodigal son in Christ's parable "came to himself" while still in a far country; and St. Mary of Egypt, the fourth-century former harlot who traveled through northern Africa seducing as many men as would have her, found a loving God waiting in the distant reaches of her depravity. Before their holy moments, both these sinners lived without lasting satisfaction. Craving fulfillment, they settled for indulgence. But each discovered the destitution of an unlimited appetite when confronted with the very stability from which they were running: the prodigal son remembered his home; St. Mary found her home in a life of repentance after meeting God in an icon of the Theotokos.

One revelation in these sacred stories is that the journey from chaos to order is possible. Hagiography is heavy with men and women who were champions of vice on one page only to be redeemed into principals of virtue on another. That's good news to many pilgrims who have traveled far and wide—physically and spiritually. We have learned that the ugliest and darkest pages from our diaries cannot keep us from the church, because nothing can separate us from the love of God.

And according to St. Herman of Alaska, nothing should separate us from loving God in return. This Russian missionary to America was, like St. Serapion, rooted in spirit but restless on foot. He often traveled many miles in extreme weather to meet the basic living needs of a region's indigenous population. But it was a cordial confrontation with a contrary worldview that revealed St. Herman's understanding that love for God must be rooted in the here and now.

A Russian naval vessel had docked in the port near his hut. St. Herman was invited aboard. In the dining quarters reserved for the ship's officers, a collection of the elite gathered for a meal and Herman was seated in their midst. He spent most of the meal in silence, and it was only during the group's later conversation that Herman's real contribution to the evening emerged. The captain of the ship stimulated discussion by asking each man what was most important to him. Each, in turn, spoke of his family, his career, of returning to Russia in glory, while some spoke of being the captains of their own vessels someday. Finally, after each man had had his say, they turned to Herman, who had been sitting quietly attentive. "Old man," they asked, "what is most important to you?" Herman answered, "Forgive me, brothers; from this day forward, from this hour, from this minute, let us strive to love God above all."

St. Herman's reply shakes me convincingly. He communicates to my distracted soul the great grounding principles of stability—be centered on God, and be centered on Him now. Notice St. Herman's reference to St. Paul, who wrote, "Now is the accepted time, now is the day of our salvation." The difficult task is to focus not on the God of yesterday or tomorrow, but on the God of the eternal Now. To live that fully in the moment, to love life that much, is to experience a transformation. The people and circumstances immediately before me, though they may not change, may grow more radiant because I have chosen to focus on the radiant God who dwells within them. I may see my world differently because I become a different person. I become a focused, theocentric person.

The woman from the village, St. Serapion, the rooted nun, the prodigal son, St. Mary, St. Herman—all are aspects of stability personified. In the rest and discernment of my post-Valaam days, they are comforting guides. They haunt my anxious moments when I face the difficulty of walking away from Valaam and toward a mysterious future. And they stand quietly behind those men and women in my life now who are struggling toward the same sanctity.

From yesterday's stories to today's examples. As I survey the names and faces in my life, I am especially instructed by my new set of fellow pilgrims—those with whom I attend church. Though still a visitor in the eyes of many in this parish, I am welcomed as a new thread in a beautiful tangle of relationships that stretches back far beyond the year of my birth. We have recently entered the season of Great Lent, when the fortitude of my companions becomes a critical support to my own.

I discover in my new friends a stability of an inspiring kind, one that brings richness and depth to relationships. On the evening before the first Monday of Lent, our congregation gathers for Forgiveness Vespers. The language of the Liturgy increasingly reviews the mercy of God toward His creation. His creation, we learn, is sick and in need of serious repair. To begin Lent in a condition of spiritual health means that we are to forgive each other for our respective contributions to the cosmic illness. We are to forgive, to be forgiven, and to start Lent clean.

We hear a brief homily on the Lord's Prayer. To receive the forgiveness of God—the only key that fits the lock on heaven's door—we must confront the singular condition of being merciful to others. "Forgive us our trespasses as we forgive those who trespass against us," the prayer reads. That and a few parables from our Lord are stark reminders that the heart of stone cannot rise to meet the glories of God. Then, at the conclusion of the service, the priest steps forward to face the congregation. One by one we approach him, then move to his right, finally encircling the interior of the temple. What we say to him and to each other is only as personal as it needs to be for the cleansing act of forgiveness to do its work. We are to ask forgiveness—and to receive it—for anything said or done that has caused offense.

I am whispering this intimacy to strangers. This congregation had been my home for only a few months before I went to Valaam, and it has been a few months since my return. I recognize many faces but few names. Their voices, their families, their gifts, even their sins are unknown to me. But I immediately recognize that they are deeply known by one another. Lining these walls are men and women who grew up together, who shared life's significant events, and who will probably die in the presence of one another. And I wonder, because of the stability of these relationships that span space and time, does forgiveness have a deeper meaning for them right now than for me?

And so it was at Valaam. These brothers lived near each other, sometimes dangerously near. To be rooted in monastic life includes a daily commitment not only to religious ritual, but also to navigating the dizzying dynamics of close interaction with one's fellows. I saw in some of these men a genuine friendship—cleansed of superficial sentimentality—that was the product of a common purpose, common task, and common hardship.

And a common Lord. In truth, everyone suffers from corruption and wandering. Humanity is not only blessed with magnificent nobility, but burdened with sinfulness. Our nobility is obscured from shining brilliantly. We know this. We feel the effects of the fall of man intimately, frequently, painfully. The habit of humanity is to seek peace and permanence in fragile and foolish constructions—worldly diversions, fleshly indulgences, devilish autonomy. But at least we are seeking.

The stability we crave, though, is the sole possession and

gift of Him who is the same yesterday, today, and forever. He is the centering Love that fills our spinning world. And He has placed a burning candle in the window of His Church, inviting us who are lost and hungry and wandering. It is the same Church that has remained stable in the face of every turbulent age as "the pillar and ground of the truth" (1 Timothy 3:15). Every soul in her membership is graced with access to the sacred stability that is Christ Himself, to Him who settles souls. St. Paul, in his epistle to seekers in Ephesus, describes the holy sheltering in this way:

> Now, therefore, you are no longer strangers and foreigners, but fellow citizens with the saints and members of the household of God, having been built on the foundation of the apostles and prophets, Jesus Christ Himself being the chief corner stone, in whom the whole building, being joined together, grows into a holy temple in the Lord, in whom you also are being built together for a dwelling place of God in the Spirit (2:19–22).

CHAPTER 17

THE STORY

The curtains fill with faint breeze and tease away from the open window, then hang still again. I cannot sleep. In several minutes the clock beside my bed will ring as I have programmed it to do. I hear no sound but the soft rustle of swaying leaves. Time has passed unnoticed. It is night—one hour before the Easter Pascha Liturgy.

I dress, then move quietly through the house. There is nothing to take to the temple but the usual—joy from the astonishing events that will unfold this night, guilt from another Lent of scattered effort, and hope of meeting Christ, who welcomes the eleventh-hour people. Somehow, though, feelings are irrelevant. Indeed, something infinitely more interesting is moving toward center stage. The dark corners in every fold of the universe rumble in anticipation as the priest readies his vestments and the choir arranges the hymns.

I pat my pockets, listening for the familiar jingle of coins and car keys. The money is needed for a meal at an all-night restaurant; the keys for transporting my hungry body there after the Liturgy. I walk through the living room, brushing with my fingertips the wall holding the icon of the Blessed Virgin Mary. Traveling light, I open the front door and step into a humid Florida night. Faint blue-and-white shades of television screens flicker from nearby homes. It is the only evidence of life I can see, and I imagine that they shine upon the bodies of sleeping men and women.

Turning south onto 56th Street, I roll down the window and inhale the warm air. The temple fills early and completely, so I've left home expecting to arrive with time to spare. Midnight is near and the streets are peppered with the flashy vessels of late Saturday revelers. Music and attitude spray from a few cars. We—all of us—are traveling toward our altars, to worship our gods, seeking relief from afflictions that feel personal and unique but are, in fact, common and everywhere.

I marvel at the ache of the soul, how it winds its way like water around the objects we place in its path. What a glorious thing. No dam of bounty, status, noise, psychology, or distraction is sufficient to protect us when the pangs of our true selves come calling. I have felt my share. And like my fellow night pilgrims, steering toward whatever they have constructed as their promised lands, I am simply trying to keep my eyes on the road and trust it takes me to a better place.

I have lived for a brief time in the warm fold of Valaam Monastery with men and women who are responding to the pangs of their true selves. They, and their spiritual ancestors, tell me that the true self is not the distorted, hollow construction of personal whim and cultural manipulation that so often meets our gaze when we look courageously into ourselves. No, the true self is the shining pearl beneath. It is the image of God that bears my name. And it is worthy of deep respect and vigorous celebration. It is worth rescuing.

As the years pass, my memories of Valaam will gradually be contained only in photographs. Even these will fade and yellow with time. The few artifacts I managed to slip past scrutiny at the border—icons, candles, an audio recording—will enter the cycle of display and replacement on mantles and shelves, and in recollections and conversations. But they will never fall out of favor. Rather, they will linger for a lifetime on the edges of my mind, fading in and out of consciousness like these streetlights that pass, one after another, through the corners of my vision as I drive through the night.

Pulling onto the highway, I settle into a legal speed. A police officer once told me I should give it a try, and tonight I am unhurried. Neon peeks through tree branches thick with greenery as I pass over twenty blocks of city streets. The breeze moves forcefully now through the interior of the car, and I reach over to move an old newspaper from the passenger seat to the floor. Resisting the urge to turn on the radio, I labor instead to listen to nothing more than rushing wind and random thoughts.

When I arrive at the church, the nave will be dark. We are still squarely on this side of the Resurrection. The stone has not been moved and many of us have only to look toward our chests to find it. We feebly commiserate with the disciples and their shattering confusion. You go through life placing your trust in anything that promises a decent return. Then, one Person appears in whom you invest every shred of your being. He gave eternal life; did they feel foolish for that brief time when He was dead and gone? At least we know what awaits on the next page of the story. Compared to that of the disciples, perhaps the intensity of our joy is dimmed because of it.

I have known the Story since childhood. That fixed point in spring—yes, shifting dates but always present and waiting—when flowers and clothing and sins turn white. The Story was recounted faithfully in the churches of my youth, in the wild variety of flannelboard figures, song titles, hymn selections, Sunday school handouts, real wooden crosses, and fancy dramatizations. Some years we awoke and celebrated before dawn. The Story was always told.

And always believed. The nave will be dark when I arrive but will not remain so. Even as the night set hard on my family when my parents finally chose fresh and separate lives for themselves, the darkness never lasted. Grace entered when I needed it most, in the form of a book or a friend or a movie or a walk in the woods. And I think grace entered my parents' lives also, as my sister and I emerged shaken but poised and resilient.

There were forays into cultures beyond the one I inherited. Shades of wildness and freedom colored my youth. Discovering that I could make music and be joyful, attend college on the other side of the country, sample life in its strange but exciting forms, visit other countries, appreciate other faiths— all this was powerfully shaping. A wider worldview was being forged from such exposure. And there in every shadow formed by new sights and new lights, the Story remained.

Then I entered Orthodoxy, and something happened to the Story. Or, rather, something happened to me: I no longer observed, I *entered.* I now walk with Christ in real time—day by day, through the Passion Week. The liturgical services contain the pious reflections of saints and hymn-writers, filling the biblical accounts with rich detail. I stand among His disciples listening to their thoughts. His Mother's heart opens and her anguish and hope are revealed. His cross is stained with fresh blood. I identify with Judas, even secretly respecting him because at least he held out for thirty pieces of silver, when I so often betray Christ for less. The liturgies vigorously discard sentimentality and explore real people in real events with real consequences.

Tonight, I travel toward my first Pascha service since

returning from Valaam Monastery. The warriors there challenged me to keep the Story present and near. Do not trivialize its heroes by treating them as magical figures in a mythological sphere. No, they, and those since who have loved the Story, attained Christ by constantly grappling with the crude matter of their immediate circumstances. They were laborers whose redemptive scope included nothing beyond the simple materials—the persons, the tasks, the hour—before them.

I emerged from Valaam with this: *I am not my own, but belong to God, who loved me into being.* Moving through this evening, I imagine a different world. Not a pure and polished Planet of Eden, but simply a life closer to the prayerful one I encountered at the monastery. Monks are imperfect, as imperfect as any of us, and they fall as hard and as often. Still, there, a person lives not for himself, but for his Lord and his brother; there, to work is to participate with God in His creativity; there, sin is not as worrisome as not repenting; there, rest is a treasured part of the weekly routine; and there, they rise when fallen. Our culture needs plenty of all of this. We need the healing that these tedious, boring, difficult, but life-giving disciplines can bring. Valaam is an oasis of clarity for a world of confusion. Valaam is an island for America.

The details of my pilgrimage may fade, but the monastic experience has, by the grace of God, taken root; it will offer occasional nourishment for the journey and shade for the times when I feel like quitting. But it is only one step in that journey. It is a special grace among a host of mercies the Lord has granted to this pilgrim. The event will fade as it should, but the mysteries it imparted will grow and be fruitful. In that way, each of us has events and mysteries uniquely our own but drawing us toward a shared and holy communion.

And it is in Christ, after all, that we discover our true selves.

Crushing our defenses, His cross; granting us abundant life, His death; illuminating every speck and sliver of creation with love, His Resurrection. I travel this highway tonight trying to turn from every thought that might drain the Story of its power over me. And they come as they always will come. But I drive with the winds of mercy, keeping my eyes on the road and trusting it takes me to a better place.

There, rising in the distance like a dim gray cloud, is the church. Palm trees line the road and sway gently under a black night sky hanging low. Scores of red taillights flutter, following their drivers as each finds a resting place. In a few moments, we will enter the Story. What we often consider to be the last chapter we will experience as the first breath of new life. I walk toward the door with my eyes to the earth, seeing only the ground that will hold my next step. Suddenly, the choir's pure song pulls at the wind, and in this moment everything I have been and ever will be does not resist, but turns and enters.

EPILOGUE

BY FATHER JONAH PAFFHAUSEN

N ow, in 2003, the monastery buildings have passed almost completely into the hands of the Brother hood. There are over one hundred fifty monks, five functioning sketes, and eight or more *podvorya* (urban priories). The zealotry and insecurity of the brothers, under the firm and kind guidance of Fr. Pankratiy, have been transformed into warmth and maturity, love and patience. I have been back several times over the past ten years and seen the transformation.

The building pilgrimage was for six weeks in the summer, under the midnight sun. There is nothing, however, like Valaam in the depths of winter . . .

The building at the Skete of the Forerunner was finished by the monastery, and there are two hermits and two novices living there in profound stillness. I even had the blessing to serve the Liturgy in the tiny chapel in the building that our groups began to build. I could not help but wonder how many saints would serve at that altar, and even I could stand there in their midst, and partake of a little of the grace they had acquired.

When I was there in November of 2002, we had the opportunity to meet and talk with one of the hermits, Father Isaakiy, who had been in the Caucasus for twenty-five years, and now for ten at Valaam. There I encountered, again, a man of the most profound spiritual vision and maturity, and yet an intellectual of great learning. We spoke for hours about the holy Elder Sophrony's vision of the transformative process of growth towards spiritual maturity, from being enwrapped in our own selfish individualism to becoming an authentic person. Then to the transcendence of that in the hypostatic principle, in which we embrace others in our own personal "I"— the realization of communion.

Even here in the depths of the wilderness, hundreds of miles from any city, was a man who embraces the whole world in himself in love, interceding for the world. The project of the building, through serving this holy man, was somehow fulfilled.

Fr. Raphael, tiny, frail, and physically very weak, could not endure the climate of Valaam, at 62 degrees north latitude. He moved to Mount Athos, to a skete near the Bulgarian monastery. Later, he returned to the Russian Caucasus near Sochi, with several monastic communities who look to his guidance, where he remains.

The greatest impact, however, was the impact on the young men and women who went to Valaam in that summer nine years ago. It was a defining moment for their lives, in which they encountered both Christ and themselves through their efforts, their sacrifice, and through the elder. Whatever course the lives of each of those fifty-plus people will take, Valaam remains firmly etched in their memories, an encounter with an earthly heaven and an angelic man.

NOTES

1 Matthew the Poor, *The Communion of Love*. Crestwood, NY: SVS Press, 1984, p. 16.

2 St. Augustine, *Confessions*. New York: Penguin Books, 1961, p. 21.

3 C. S. Lewis, *The Screwtape Letters*. New York: MacMillan, 1961, p. 38.

4 Tennyson, Alfred Lord, "Ulysses." *Victorian Prose and Poetry*, ed. Lionel Trilling and Harold Bloom. New York: Oxford University Press, 1973, p. 418.

5 St. John Chrysostom, *On Eutropios*, Homily 2.6.

6 Henry David Thoreau, *Walden and Other Writings of Henry David Thoreau*, New York: The Modern Library, 1937, p. 83.

7 St. John Climacus, *The Ladder of Divine Ascent*, ¶17.1. Boston: Holy Transfiguration Monastery, 1991, p. 122.

8 St. John Climacus, op. cit., ¶17.6, p. 123.

9 Jim Forest, *The Ladder of the Beatitudes*. Maryknoll, NY: Orbis Books, 1999, p. 22.

10 G. K. Chesterton, *What's Wrong with the World*. London: Cassell and Company, 1910, chapter 5.

11 Alexander Schmemann, *Great Lent*. Crestwood, NY: SVS Press, 1990, p. 36.

12 Thomas Merton, *A Search for Solitude*. San Francisco: Harper, 1977.

13 St. John Climacus, *op. cit.*, ¶15.20, p. 106.

14 Amma Syncletica, in *The Sayings of the Desert Fathers*. Tr. Benedicta Ward. Kalamazoo, MI: Cistercian Publications, 1975, p. 234.

15 Abba Milos, in *The Sayings of the Desert Fathers*. London: Cistercian Publications, 1975, p. 150.

16 Archimandrite Sophrony, *St Silouan the Athonite*. Crestwood, NY: SVS Press, 1999, p. 422.

ABOUT THE AUTHOR

John Oliver received his B.A. in English from Malone College in Canton, Ohio, and is currently earning his M. Div. from St. Tikhon's Orthodox Theological Seminary in South Canaan, Pennsylvania. His work on Christianity and ecology has appeared in journals such as *Touchstone* and *Praxis,* and he is an accomplished musician. John is the husband of Lara and the proud father of Anastasia and Genevieve.

MUSIC FROM VALAAM MONASTERY

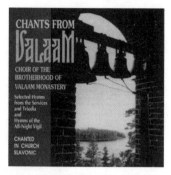

CHANTS FROM VALAAM

In Church Slavonic
By the choir of Old Valaam
Monastery in Russia.
Selected hymns from the
services and Triodia and hymns
of the all-night vigil.
CD—
Order No. 000068—$16.95*
Cassette—
Order No. 000067—$11.95*

TASTE THE FOUNTAIN OF IMMORTALITY

In English
By the choir of Old Valaam
Monastery in Russia.
Featuring ancient Russian,
Byzantine, and Georgian chants.
CD Only—
Order No. 002821—$16.95*

Thirsting for God in a Land of Shallow Wells
by Matthew Gallatin

Beginning in the street ministry days of the Jesus Movement, Matthew Gallatin devoted more than twenty years to evangelical Christian ministry. He was a singer/songwriter, worship leader, youth leader, and Calvary Chapel pastor. Nevertheless, he eventually accepted a painful reality: no matter how hard he tried, he was never able to experience the God whom he longed to know. His was a great dream that could not find fulfillment, a deep question that could not answer itself, an eternal thirst dwelling in a land of shallow wells.

In *Thirsting for God,* philosophy professor Gallatin expresses many of the struggles that a Protestant will encounter in coming face to face with Orthodoxy: such things as Protestant relativism, rationalism versus the Orthodox sacramental path to God, and the unity of Scripture and Tradition. He also discusses praying with icons, praying written prayers, and many other Orthodox traditions.

An outstanding book that will help Orthodox readers more deeply appreciate their faith, and will give Protestant readers a more thorough understanding of the Church.

Paperback, 192 pages (ISBN 1-888212-28-4) Order No. 005216—$14.95*

An Englishman in the Court of the Tsar:
The Spiritual Journey of Charles Sydney Gibbes
by Christine Benagh

Demoralized by the encroaching liberalism of the Anglican Church in the early twentieth century, Englishman Charles Sydney Gibbes travels abroad in a crisis of faith. Finding work as a tutor to the Russian aristocracy, his world is changed forever when he becomes a tutor to the Empress' children. Following the royal family to Siberia and later continuing on to China, Gibbes eventually returns full circle to Great Britain, there dedicating his life as an Orthodox priest to the memory of the Imperial Family, and the faith he discovered in their distant homeland.

Hardcover, 304 pages (includes 8-page photo section) (ISBN 1-888212-19-5) Order No. 004749—$24.95*

Becoming Orthodox
by Fr. Peter E. Gillquist
The inspiring story of over two thousand evangelical Christians and their search for historic Christianity. This book is for evangelical Christians on their own search for the Church and for Orthodox Christians looking for renewal. Contains answers to common Protestant concerns such as: why we worship the way we do, "Call no man father," and "Facing up to Mary." Paperback, 191 pages (ISBN 0-9622713-3-0) Order No. 000049—$13.95*

A Faith Fulfilled
by Fr. Michael Harper
Michael Harper, known to many American Christians as a longtime leader in the evangelical and charismatic movements, now comes before us in a new role: as a convert to the Orthodox Church.
Paperback, 240 pages (ISBN 1-888212-12-8) Order No. 004514—$13.95*

Our Hearts' True Home
edited by Virginia Nieuwsma
Our Hearts' True Home presents fourteen warm, inspiring stories of women coming into the Orthodox Faith. These women come from a wide variety of backgrounds, yet there's a common thread: no matter how they struggled, their journeys are infused with the love and mercy of God.
Paperback, 178 pages (ISBN 1-888212-02-0) Order No. 002109—$12.95*

Anglican-Orthodox Pilgrimage
edited by Franklin Billerbeck
Why are so many Anglicans considering entrance into the Orthodox Church? Written entirely by former Anglicans/Episcopalians, this book contains a strong apologetic for the Orthodox Faith as well as personal testimonies by those who have recently made the pilgrimage.
Paperback, 72 pages (ISBN 0-9622713-5-7) Order No. 000057—$4.50*

* Prices do not include shipping and handling or applicable sales tax.

To request a Conciliar Press catalog of other introductory books about the Orthodox Faith and Church life, to place a credit card order, or to obtain current ordering information, please call Conciliar Press at either (800) 967-7377 or (831) 336-5118, or log on to our website: www.conciliarpress.com